Peace-Weavers
and Shield-Maidens

Women in Early English Society

Kathleen Herbert

GW00771359

Anglo-Saxon Books

BY THE SAME AUTHOR

English Heroic Legends
Looking for the Lost Gods of England
Queen of Lightning
Ghost in the Sunlight
Bride of the Spear

First Published 1997
Reprinted 1999/2002

Published by
Anglo-Saxon Books
Frithgarth, Thetford Forest Park
Hockwold-cum-Wilton
Norfolk, England

Printed by
Antony Rowe Ltd.
Chippenham
Wiltshire, England

The cover drawing is by Brian Partridge.

A Cataloguing-in-Publication record for this book
is available from the British Library.

ISBN 1–898281–11–4

Contents

Foreword..4

Introduction...5

Text...7

Bibliography..57

Foreword

Kathleen Herbert read English at Oxford where she heard Tolkien's lectures; as a result she has been working with Old English literature and early English culture ever since. She is particularly interested in the relationship between history and the creative imagination, and has explored this in lectures and articles, also in historical novels and short stories.

The following text is a transcript of a talk given by Kathleen Herbert to a meeting of Þa Engliscan Gesiþas (The English Companions).

Details of Þa Engliscan Gesiþas can be found at the back of this book.

Introduction

There are still too many people who seem to think that English life began on October 14th 1066. As the earliest surviving account of the English was published in 98, this fixation on 1066 robs the victims of at least half of their communal life history – the time when the language was formed, social patterns were shaped, customs and laws were established and tried out, ideas and emotions were given voice and memory in songs and stories.

To ignore, and so forget one's earliest historical records is to be as deprived as to lose one's memory. When that happens, the sufferer cannot fully understand and cope with the present.

The first recorded statement about the English was made by the Roman historian Cornelius Tacitus in *Germania*. For him, the note-worthy fact about the *Anglii* was that they were members of an alliance of Goddess-worshippers. The allies kept a sacred truce, disarming and merry-making, whenever their Lady came to visit them. Then, when She departed, knowing that the blessings of peace demand sacrifice, they killed the dedicated servants who had ministered to Her.

If this is really the earliest reference to the English in European history, and not merely the first to survive, then it makes an appropriate opening to an account of the earliest Englishwomen, the part they played in the making of England, what they did in peace and war, the impressions they left at home and on the continent, how they were recorded in the chronicles, how they come alive in heroic verse and jokes.

The poet and novelist George Meredith said that every society must have its civilisation judged by the way it treats its women: what happens in bodily fact, and also what is said, felt, imagined and fantasised by and about them. Sometimes there is a wide gap between fact and fancy. Some cultures have created countless legends about immortal females – nymphs and queens of faerie, with dazzling beauty and magical generosity – while their own flesh-and-blood womenfolk get sexually bullied and mentally stunted.

There is enough material of different kinds remaining from early England for readers of the twentieth and twenty-first centuries to make up their own minds about what the women were like. We can, for example, compare the history and the poetry, to see if they are telling similar stories and showing the same kinds of women. One advantage of their long neglect by the mass media and in the popular imagination, is that their stories have not become stale or trivialised. Also, they have not been distorted in our minds by the social or political fashions of the centuries that stretch between them and ourselves.

The most striking impression I get from this material is how fresh, how vivid and lively it seems to me. I enjoy reading about these women; they seem to have made the most of their opportunities, even when luck was against them. My second reaction came as a surprise at first – what I was reading did not seem unfamiliar to me. I knew these women, even though they lived so far away in the past; I could recognise ideas, feelings, situations, even turns of phrase that I had met before in later periods of our history, even our own time. 'Anglo-Saxon' England is not alien territory, beyond our mental frontiers and difficult to visit. These records are part of our own life story.

Note: Early written records made by the English, or about them, were in Old English, Latin or Greek. In this book, quotations from these works are given in Modern English, with the sources named in the notes. There has been some unavoidable inconsistency in the spelling of early English proper names. I decided to compromise, for the sake of readers who are not familiar with early names and Old English orthography. I have kept the names as used in whichever source I happened to be quoting, so that they can be recognised while following up the references. The vowel symbol 'æ' has been used, but not the consonants 'þ', 'ð' and 'Ƿ', in case they were mistaken by the uninitiated as ancient forms of 'd' and 'p'.

No one can enjoy the rich flavour of early English talk without hearing and speaking in Old English. We can still relish the echoes of it in lively regional speech, pungent and mouth-filling. There are excellent guides to the primal English language, also to rune-lore. It does not take long to feel at home in both of them.

Peace-Weavers and Shield-Maidens: Women in Early English Society

A line or two in an old song, the gleam of garnets set in a gold brooch that was last worn more than fourteen hundred years ago, the look and feel of a pattern-welded sword –these things can all cast a spell. They speak to us about ancient Germania.[1]

In the enchanting world of the legends, the Peace-Weaver and the Shield-Maiden stand over against each other, utterly unlike. To the right hand is the Shield-Maiden – the fierce virgin who keeps all men at her spear's length distant, or only comes to closer quarters with her spear or axe. On the left hand is the Peace-Weaver – the royal bride who holds out her hands in welcome to bring warring tribes together in friendship at her wedding feast.

The Peace-Weaver and the Shield-Maiden are names to conjure with. The two are such powerful archetypes because they rise from people's collective experiences, memories, dreams. Therefore they need to be evoked very warily. An archetypal image ought to be a living source of inspiration – but it can be stamped into a dead, and deadly, cliché.

So, after calling up the radiant images of the Peace-Weaver and the Shield-Maiden, it is useful to think about the first[2] English girl to be recorded in European history.

---

[1] Any comment about the early English has to start with Tacitus, as his study of the German lands and the Germanic tribes is the first book to mention them. Obviously, he studies, interprets and writes with a Roman mind and in the Latin language; also, he has political aims and prejudices that belong to Rome rather than Germania. With all these considerations, what he writes tallies with other evidence.
Tacitus: *Germania* ch. 2–27. A general survey of the people, their religion, customs and social life.

[2] When reading any comments about this early period, whenever words such as 'first', 'only', 'never' etc. are used, the reader must always mentally add: 'So far as we

Her story was written down by Procopius, a high-ranking official in the Emperor Justinian's civil service, in his history of the Gothic War of 535–552. Procopius got his details about the English princess from some member of a Frankish embassy. She stepped out onto the European stage at some time during the years between 533 and 548, while Theudebert I was King of the eastern Franks. Procopius finished his book by about 558. This is not a legend of by-gone days for him; the girl was his contemporary.[3]

Five hundred years before he told the story of the English girl, her people the Engle (Latin: Anglii) were living on the 'neck' of the Jutland Peninsula. There is no evidence that they had ever been living anywhere else in the remoter past.[4] The seven tribes of the peninsula and the near-by islands were bound in a holy alliance: they all worshipped Nerthuz, Mother Earth, as their Great Goddess. One of these allied tribes was called the Wærne (Latin: Varini).

Five hundred years had brought violent changes to all the Germanic peoples. When Procopius made his notes about the 'Angiloi',[5] most of them had already settled in the eastern part of the one-time Roman province of Britannia. The 'Varni', also heading westwards, had arrived near the mouth of the Rhine, on the eastern side. On the western side

---

know'. So much evidence has been destroyed, so much may still be waiting to be discovered.

[3] Procopius: *The History of the Wars* Book VIII ch. 20. This book is part of the Gothic War. The Eastern Roman Empire was attempting to re-conquer the Western imperial provinces and Italy; Procopius was serving on the staff of the Commander-in-Chief, Belisarius. The Goths were difficult enemies; they could retreat to the Alpine passes, also get reinforcements from the north. The Byzantines needed an ally to take the Goths from the north. The only powerful Germanic nation that was also Catholic was the Franks. Neither side trusted the other. The story of the English princess came into Greek history during these negotiations. The Franks wanted to push up the price by magnifying their power and influence. In III ch. 20. they are claiming that they control Britain. The Byzantines were not naive; Procopius was too polite to put on record that his allies were boastful liars. His story of how a force from England, led by a girl, sailed to the borders of Frankia and ordered a Merovingian princess, the sister of King Theudebert, to end her marriage and go home, says it all.

[4] Tacitus: *Germania* ch. 40: the Anglii; ch. 2: the Germanic tribes as indigenous.

[5] I have kept the forms of the names Procopius used when telling his story in Bk. VIII, 20.

were the Franks – uneasy neighbours, since there were so many more of them. They were fierce, powerful and aggressive; it was dangerous to annoy them.

Hermegisclus, King of the Varni, did what he could to safeguard his people. His first wife had just died; they had one son, Radigis, who was just old enough to go into battle but was not yet married, or even promised. He was probably in his early to middle teens.

Hermegisclus himself offered marriage to Theudechild, younger half-sister of the Frankish King Theudebert I. This might keep him on peaceful terms with the Franks for the time being. It might cause trouble for Radigis later on, to have a half-Frankish step-brother as a rival, backed by a Frankish step-mother and her kinsfolk. So Hermegisclus also sent messengers to Britain, asking for the English King's sister[6] as a bride for Radigis. This would secure a friendly ally across the North Sea, and also a safe exile for the boy if the Franks turned on him.

These plans went well at first. Theudechild arrived from Frankia as the new queen. The English King's sister officially betrothed herself to Radigis by accepting the large sum of gold that Hermegisclus had sent as a bride-gift. Betrothal marked the beginning of wedlock not a free trial period to see whether the couple felt it worth going on. They were pledging themselves for life; Procopius commented that in German eyes, taking the gold counted morally and legally as having had sexual intercourse with the bridegroom.

---

[6] Which English King? Can the name *Engle* be taken literally? The Jutes and the Saxons were nearer neighbours. Archaeology shows that there were very close connections between the Franks and the Jutes; Saxons were operating in Gaul along the Loire at the time of Childeric (d. 481) according to Gregory of Tours. They figure in his History till the end of the sixth century. The Franks would know Saxons and Jutes and could name them accurately if they chose. The English were further away in Britain, but they could know of them through traffic by sea and also through their relations with the Varini. Their nearest king would be one of the East Anglian dynasty, the *Wuffingas*, whose royal hall was at Rendlesham and whose noble dead were buried at Sutton Hoo. The treasure found there draws the imagination to them. Further north were the *Icelingas* who claimed descent from Offa of Angeln, and might well claim to be the highest English royal race. Their descendant, Offa of Mercia certainly thought so. All this has nothing to do with history as far as we know at present. *The Origins of England 410–600*, M. J. Whittock, Croom Helm 1986. See ch. 4 pp. 161–77; Appendix 1, Lists C & G.

Not long after the marriage – too soon to get his new wife with child, or for the English girl to set out on her wedding journey – Hermegisclus went out riding with his hearth-companions. A bird was sitting on a tree; it croaked noisily at him. The king turned to his companions, saying the bird had just told him that he had only forty more days to live. The Franks found this too natural for comment; they knew that the bird was a raven, and Who had sent the message. Procopius tried to find a rational Greek explanation that would satisfy his mind; he suggested that the king knew all about his failing health and invented the story about the talking bird to cloak his political arrangements with supernatural awe.

The king took the news calmly. He spent his last days making plans with his nobles, looking for ways to keep his young son and his folk out of danger when he was dead. He pointed out that his English allies would have a long and difficult sea-voyage to bring help to the Varni. On the other hand, the Franks were just across the Rhine; they had all the power they needed ready at hand to protect the Varni or smash them – and there was no doubt which they would prefer, unless they were kept in a friendly mood by another marriage alliance. So the king said that Radigis must give his word to marry his step-mother.[7]

Exactly forty days after the bird's message, Hermegisclus died. Radigis married Theudechild without Frankish objections. A message came to the English girl that her wedding was off, but she could keep the gold to compensate her for the public snub.

From this point in the story, 'the island girl' took events into her own hands. Her kinsfolk certainly backed her all the way, but she not only directed what was done but saw to it personally. First, she wanted an explanation. When she did not get one, she wanted revenge not money. She collected ships and fighting men. (Procopius says 400 ships and 100,000 warriors; either he had confused the Germanic numerals, or the

---

[7] An ancient and honourable Germanic practice with sound political reasons – if a royal wife had been efficiently peace-weaving, it could be awkward if she went back to her family and made an alliance with someone else, possibly an enemy. There is an example in Kent just after the Conversion (Bede: *Historia Ecclesiastica Gentis Anglorum*, Bk. II, ch. 5) but it also happened in Christian Wessex in 858. King Alfred's eldest brother married his Frankish step-mother after the death of their father, King Ethelwulf. (Asser, *Life of Alfred*, ch. 17)

Franks were exaggerating the northern hordes that they could bring for or against the Eastern Empire. Four ships like the one buried at Sutton Hoo, with about a hundred warriors to handle them, would be a useful force.)

And so the English, with 'the island girl' at their head, went back to invade Europe.

The story makes clear that though the girl took a younger brother to second her, she was the war-leader who gave the orders. It is therefore very important to note what her first order was, when they came to land on the continent. She had been woundingly insulted and had come to avenge her good name, but she was not blind to everything except the need to glut her rage. She told her men to stay where they landed until they had built a strong fort close to the Rhinemouth. She made her headquarters there; she would not risk having her ships burned or captured. Nor would she make the mistake of letting her troops be cut off and trapped inland, unable to get back to the ships or to get help from them.

About twenty years earlier, the Geatish king, Hygelac, had been trapped like that at the Rhinemouth.[8] He was cut down; his bones were kept on display among the Franks. His nephew, the famous hero Beowulf, had to swim for his life. The war-leader who had brought up the Frankish troops so fast and smashed the Geatish raiders was Theudebert, before he succeeded his father as king. The English girl was challenging the same power in the same place; her truant bridegroom had just married Theudebert's sister.

When she was ready to move, she sent her brother to find the Varnian forces. They were encamped not far from the shore, where the Rhine meets the open sea. The English gave battle at once, trounced the Varni and killed a lot of them; the rest, including the young king, fled. The English chased them for a while, but had the sense to turn back to their camp to report. If they expected to be thanked, they had a shock. Their

---

[8] *Beowulf* ed. Klaeber (Heath and Co., Massachusetts, 1950): Intro. pp.xxxix-xl; for textual references see Glossary of Proper Names pp.433–44. For links between the story of Beowulf and the Anglian kingdoms in Britain see *The Origins of Beowulf and the pre-Viking Kingdom of East Anglia*: S. Newton, Brewer 1993; also *Beowulf* ll.1931-61 and Note on Offa.

Had 'the island girl' listened to the scops singing about the disaster at Rhinemouth or had she just worked out her own campaign by her own intelligence?

leader gave them a sharp rebuke for wasting their time: why had they not brought Radigis to her alive? She gave the sharpest tongue-lashing to her brother. Then she sent out a hand-picked force to hunt Radigis, telling them not to come back without him.

They combed the country till they found him lurking in a tract of densely-forested land, tied him up and dragged him to his betrothed. He was shaking. He was very young; he had just been defeated. Perhaps he was wounded; certainly he was exhausted, hungry and manhandled. It was not easy to be heroic. He waited for the girl to curse him, then tell her men how she wanted him killed.

She asked him quietly why he had broken the engagement that he had asked her to make; she had not been unfaithful or done him any wrong. Why had he deserted her for another woman?

He went to pieces, pleading for her mercy, blaming everyone else he could think of: he had not meant to insult her – it was his father – it was the nobles – they had told him to do it – and if she would only let him live and marry her, he would prove how well he would behave!

At this point in the story one feels sorry for the English girl, listening to this with her men standing round watching the exhibition. But she had taken gold as a pledge to marry Radigis; she had demanded that he should keep his word, for her honour's sake. This was what she had come for, this was what she had got. She kept command of herself. When the terrified gibbering stopped, she told her men to untie him and treat him kindly, now he had pledged his word to her in person. He lost no time in sending Theudechild back to Frankia. The English girl lost no time in taking her place as Queen of the Varni.

Procopius leaves it at that: 'this is how it happened'. No one ever said that she and Radigis lived happily ever after. However, their alliance survived for a long time after. In the ninth century, the continental Anglii and the Varini were still living together and sharing the same law-code.[9]

Should the first English woman in history be described as a shield-maiden who fought with prudence and mercy – or a peace-weaver who set to work with swords and slaughter?

---

[9] In a code of wergilds compiled under the Carolingians, their names are listed jointly: 'Lex Angliorum et Werinorum'. By that time, both groups were classed with Thuringians.

This story is not English: it was told by Franks and written in Greek. However, we can only begin to know people when we can listen to them speaking for themselves, even if we have to listen with the mind's ear across a distance of many centuries. Most of the remaining material in this paper comes from English sources. As far as possible their own statements have been used, though they have been put into Modern English forms.

The most useful words to hear first are some of their words for women, because these hold the basic ideas about them, built into the very fabric of the language. They come into everything else the early English said on the subject of women.

If you could ask someone from early England: *What is a woman?* the first answer would likely be: *A woman is a man, of course!*

That would not mean that Englishwomen were regarded as a sub-group of the male sex, or that they had no separate identity or personality but only a particular use. In the Germanic languages, *mann* means a human being of either sex, a member of humankind. So, in a land lease granted by a Bishop of Worcester for the duration of three lives: 'Elfweard was the first man and now it [the land] is in the hands of his daughter and she is the second man.' Early English legal documents – wills, charters, law-suits – make this meaning of *man* quite clear. They also make it clear that females owned and disposed of their own property and estates.

People (*menn*) were *wæponedmenn* or *wæpmenn* and *wifmenn*: 'weapon-people' and 'wife-people'. When they left out the idea of common humanity, *menn*, the early English classified people as *weras* and *wīfas*: 'males' and 'wives'.

A *wer* – the word survives in werewolf – was someone who could put seed into a woman so that she could make children. The word comes from the same root as the Latin *vir*, from which we get 'virile' and 'virility'. A male was distinguished by having a prick and using weapons. There has always been a very close connection between the two attributes. A Capulet retainer brags about different ways he will overcome the men and women of the Montagues, the enemy household: – 'when I have fought with the men I will be civil to the maids, I will cut off their heads... or their maidenheads... My naked weapon is out.' The same type of innuendo was being used in the Exeter Book riddles six hundred years earlier.[10]

Though *wif* is the ancestor of 'wife', it does not mean a female bound in wedlock. A fishwife, an alewife, a henwife, a housewife – these were women who had particular jobs that needed special skills. The word *wif* cannot be traced in any form in the other Indo-European languages outside Germanic. It is found in all the Germanic languages except Gothic. The entry in the Oxford English Dictionary says that it is "of obscure origin". Perhaps it is so old that its links had become obscured by time; perhaps the train of thought was so obvious that it needed no early comment. It seems very likely that the form of the word and its metaphorical images point to a connection with the verb *wefan*: 'to weave', and its related nouns *webb*: 'woven stuff' and *wefta*: 'weft', the threads crossing from side to side on a loom. Oddly, the word *wefan* is also not recorded in Gothic.

This idea of a link between weaving and woman is strengthened by considering the similar train of thought in a pair of words used in King Alfred's will. He distinguished descent in the male and the female lines as 'the spear side' and 'the spindle side'. Males expressed their masculinity by weapons; females expressed their femininity by making threads.

This Old English definition of woman as spinner and weaver was a very profound concept with several levels of meaning, from an everyday task that met a physical need, rising through art and the structure of society, up to the nature of heaven and earth.

Women clothed humankind: in the days before textile factories and the ready-made clothing trade, they spun and wove the cloth as well as furnishing the clothes. Also, women embroidered; it was the one major skill that seems to have been practised entirely by women. Doing embroidery did not mean fiddling over the useless bits of fancy-work that bored Victorian ladies perpetrated to give themselves something to do. In early England, embroidering meant furnishing: before central heating, wall-coverings, bed-hangings and coverlets meant warmth and

---

[10] *Romeo and Juliet*: Act 1. sc. 1, ll.10-32; *The Exeter Book*, A. S. P. R. vol. 3, ll. 180-210, 229-43. *The Exeter Riddle Book* trans. with introduction by Kevin Crossley-Holland, drawings by Virgil Burnett, Folio Society 1978. See especially Riddle 62.

comfort as well as cheerfulness and beauty. That was not all. Old English embroidery was a great art-form, on a level with the prestige jewellery and weaponry that we can still see in our museums, and the illuminated manuscripts that are treasured in great libraries. There are few surviving examples of Old English embroidery in England, because the Normans carried off cartloads of it to the Continent. However, in Durham Cathedral can still be seen the embroidered stole and maniple that were found in Saint Cuthbert's tomb. These were an offering from Queen Ælfflæd, the second wife of King Edward I (or the Elder) so they were made before 916, when she died. They were probably made by the skilled embroideresses who were on the staffs of royal and noble households. Likely the queen herself and her bower-maidens took some part in the work.

Embroidery as an art form was internationally recognised as an English speciality: *opus anglicanum* – English work – is the technical term for the spectacular ecclesiastical embroidery of the later Middle Ages, which has survived in some quantity. Dr David Wilson described the Durham pieces in his great survey of Anglo-Saxon art,[11] along with metalwork, jewellery, books, carvings and architecture: he says that they are "of breathtaking brilliance and beauty".

So when early Englishmen said that a woman's time was fittingly spent at her embroidery, they might be, probably were, teasing her fondness for taking time off to gossip or go looking for attractive men. They were no more demeaning women's skill and intelligence at work, than when they said that a *scop* displayed his nature when he:

"   ...*composed a new song*[12]
in correct metre...
to weave words together, and fluently
to tell a filling tale."

Like wall-paintings, embroideries could be narrative or didactic as well as ornamental. They too told stories or gave lessons; they were just

---

[11] *Anglo-Saxon Art*: D. M. Wilson, Thames and Hudson 1984; pp.154-5 and plates 205-7. *The Golden Age of Anglo-Saxon Art*: British Museum Catalogue 1984, colour plate 3.

[12] *Beowulf* ll.870-74: *word oper fand... wordum wrixlan* as translated by Kevin Crossley-Holland.

as striking and beautiful as paintings or carvings but provided warmth and comfort as well. The widow of Byrhtnoth, hero of Maldon, the wealthy and pious Lady Ælfflæd gave a wall-hanging to the Abbey of Ely where he was buried. It showed his life's deeds: here we see this feminine art performing the same function as the poem about his last battle, which we still remember and quote.[13]

However, as well as being weavers – makers and artists in the literal sense – early English women, *wifmenn*, were also seen as spinning and weaving the threads that held societies together. One Old English word for a high-born woman who married to make or keep the peace between powerful kindreds, dynasties or tribes is *frithuwebbe*: peace-weaver. This is taking the act of weaving in a very profound religious sense. It connects the particular work of women (*spinster* and *webster* are feminine occupational names) with the work of the greatest weaver of all, *Wyrd*, the original Weaver who is also the Web.[14] *Wyrd* is the nature and destined course of the world: her name comes from the verb *weorthan*: to become. *Wyrd* is constant becoming, what happens, Fate, Destiny. *Wyrd* is a feminine noun. There is some argument whether she was regarded as a goddess, as she had no temples, shrines, ritual or sacrifices; but then, nothing that men or even the gods could do could change her. She was, is and will be. And she is a weaver: "For me fate wove this, gave this to do" *(Me þæt wyrd gewæf ond gewyrht forgeaf)*.

Besides *wif*, other Old English words used to classify female human beings also give some interesting insights into early English thought-processes on the subject.

The Gothic form of Germanic did not use any word-form related to *wif*. Instead, it had two forms of the root *qin-*: *qins* meant a woman of noble rank; *qino* was one who was common, in every sense. English has the two related words 'queen' and 'quean'. The second survived in literature until the nineteenth century; by then it had the same disapproving ring as 'housewife' when it is pronounced 'hussy'. A

---

[13] See *Warrior's Way*, S. Pollington, Blandford 1989, which sets the event in its context.
[14] See discussions by Pollington: *Warrior's Way* p. 126. *The Lost Gods of England*: Brian Branston, Thames and Hudson 1974, ch. 4 Wyrd pp. 57-71. *Wyrd*: A. Stone, Newark 1989, repr. 1991. *The Old English Riming Poem*: ed. and trans. O. D. Macrae-Gibson, Brewer 1983, see line 70.

housewife worked in her own house, whatever trade she was plying there.

It is useful to think of these early English queens and queans along with the implications of the word *freo*. A *freo* was a free-born woman, one who was born to *freodom* – 'freedom'; she could make choices and act upon them, within her sphere as queen/housewife or quean/hussy. The Latin word *liberated* has the same implications. *Freogan* means 'to set free', to liberate; but it also means to 'honour', 'love,' 'like'. Therefore, *freondas* – 'friends' – were people who freely exchanged respect, liking and love. In Old English, the words friend and friendship were not cool, almost sexless, sometimes denying any suggestion of sex ("We're just good friends.") As the early English used the words in poetry, about relationships between women and men, we have to translate *freond* as 'lover', 'beloved husband/wife'; *freondship* can be passion, sexual desire, 'romantic' love – which can be found in Old English poetry, though the word *romance* was not used in England until it was introduced by the medieval French.[15] The warmth in these words is not surprising. As a name *Freo* (like the Old High German *Frija*) is the equivalent of Venus, who was not worshipped for or with cool restraint.[16]

The other name for a high-born woman in Old English, *ides*, appears in Old Saxon as *idis*. The *Idisi*, like the Scandinavian *Disir*, were otherworldly female powers who, like the *wælcyrian*, did not rank with the high gods. In later English, such presences are called nymphs, demi-goddesses, elf-queens, fairies.

In Modern English, *freo* and *ides* are usually translated as 'lady'. The Old English ancestor of lady: *hlæfdige* seems to have derived from *hlaf*:

---

[15] See *The Husband's Message*: Exeter Book, pp. 225-26. *Three Old English Elegies* pp. 49-50 with notes and glossary, ed. R. F. Leslie, Univ. of Exeter 1988. *A Choice of Anglo-Saxon Verse*: ed. and trans. Richard Hamer, Faber and Faber 1972, pp. 76-81.

A princess gets a message from her exiled husband. She is invited to join him if she is still willing – if she remembers the vows they swore to each other when they were able "to live at home, inhabit the same country and *freondscype fremman*". The words literally mean 'to do, perform, make friendship'. A translation into Modern English(ME) would have to be 'to make <u>love</u>' or 'to show our <u>love</u> openly'. The poet was not being coy. Friendship was the expression of the deepest human emotion.

[16] See *Dictionary of Northern Mythology*: Rudolph Simek, trans. Angela Hall, Brewer 1993. See entries Frija, Friday, then follow the connections.

bread, 'loaf'. The chief woman of a household would have charge of the food supply, as house-keeper, even if she were rich enough to have many servants. The lives, comfort and status of the others, from kin and guests to slaves and beggars, depended on her.

So the early English idea of a woman, embedded in the language, shows a wide and exciting range of possibilities, all the way from holiness to whoring. The female is not a limited or inferior sex by nature, though it can be forced into unnatural limitations. In one way, women have a slight lead over men: no man can conceive a child in his womb or suckle it after birth, whereas any able-bodied woman can fight. In dire necessity, it is even possible to fight while carrying a child in the womb, or in the intervals of suckling, but it is not pleasant for the mother or advisable for the child. Therefore the early English saw the normal division of work – with apparently no sense of resentment or contempt on either side – as being between war, defence, law-enforcement and hunting wild animals for food, on one side; on the other, the arts and skills of peace-weaving in all its forms. This division is expressed in the words *wæpenmenn* and *wifmenn*.

Yet English women could not only fight but could command fighting men. The first Englishwoman in recorded history led her troops to the Rhine. Our greatest woman-general, one of the most effective leaders we ever had, commanded troops for eight years of decisive warfare, and ruled a country as well. If she had been born in any other nation, her name would be a household word, a patriotic legend and an inspiration to her fellow-countrywomen. As she was English, when her name is mentioned the response is usually, '*Who?*' Richard Humble comments: "It is typical of the English that the humiliating Norman Conquest of 1066 remains the best remembered event in their history, while the glorious English Reconquest of Edward (the Elder – 1st) 150 years earlier, remains sunk in almost total oblivion."[17]

By the end of his life, King Alfred had fought the Danes to a standstill and a peace treaty that would only last as long as the English could hold their frontiers. The Danes had taken root in east Englia; they controlled the east Midlands from their Five Boroughs: Stamford, Leicester,

---

[17] *The Saxon Kings*: Richard Humble, Weidenfeld and Nicholson 1980, ch. 3, p. 71.

Lincoln, Nottingham and Derby. Beyond the Humber was the Danish Kingdom of York. The whole east coast was wide open to Danish reinforcements. Up in Northumbria there was an English enclave centred on Bamburgh, but there could be little help given or taken between its lords and Wessex. Cumbria, once Northumbrian, was now part of the Kingdom of Strathclyde and was under attack from Norse Vikings from the Isles and Ireland. So 'English England' was less than half what it had been during the Viking incursions. Alfred's children were determined to win back the lost lands.

Æthelflæd[18] was King Alfred's eldest child, King Edward's sister. The Reconquest was her work as much as his. Strangely, in her case the 'oblivion' that Humble complains about was deliberate. It was willed by

---

[18] The sources for reconstructing Æthelflæd's life are:
A. Early
Life of Alfred the Great: Asser, trans. with an introduction and notes by Simon Keynes and Michael Lapidge in Alfred the Great, Penguin Classics 1983. *The Will of King Alfred*: ibid. pp. 175-7? and notes pp. 313-23. *The Anglo-Saxon Chronicle*: trans. with introduction and notes by G. A. Garmonsway, Dent 1972. Versions C (Abingdon), D (Worcester) and E (Peterborough) for the years 909/10-18 (pp. 94-105).
It can at first be harassing to keep switching between the different versions of the Chronicle. The reader may find it easier to start with one of the composite summaries given by modern historians and then go back to the Chronicle.
B. Medieval Latin Historians and Chroniclers
Henry of Huntingdon (1084-1155): *Historia Anglorum* trans. as *The Chronicle of Henry of Huntingdon*, Llanerch Press 1991, see pp. 163-68: years 906-22.
Florence of Worcester (d. 1118): *Chronicon ex Chronicis*: trans. as *A History of the Kings of England*, Llanerch, see pp. 71-8: years 901-20.
William of Malmesbury (d. 1143): *Gesta Regum Anglorum I*: trans. as *The Kings before the Norman Conquest*, Llanerch, see ch. 125 pp. 108-9.
C. Modern historical work
Anglo-Saxon England: ch. X The Conquest of Scandinavian England: F. M. Stenton, O.U.P. 1975.
Æthelflæd, Lady of the Mercians: F. T. Wainwright in *The Anglo-Saxons: Studies in some aspects of their History and Culture presented to Bruce Dickens* ed. P. Clemoes. Bowes & Bowes 1959 reprinted in *Scandinavian England* (Chichester 1975) pp. 305–24.
Women in Anglo-Saxon England: Christine Fell, British Museum Publications 1984, ch. 5 Manor and Court.
Women Warlords: Tim Newark, Blandford 1989, ch. 5 Women of Christ.
The Saxon Kings: Richard Humble, Weidenfeld and Nicolson 1980, ch. 3 Edward 'the Elder'.

her own family; I believe that it could not have fallen on her without her own knowledge and consent.

During the 880's, her father arranged her marriage with Æthelred, the Ealdorman of West Mercia, English Mercia, that remnant of the once-mighty kingdom that had not fallen into Danish hands. Æthelred was keeping up a valiant and effective resistance. He had proved a faithful ally to Alfred and Edward; in 886, they had re-taken London. Alfred trusted so completely in the Mercian Lord's political and military reliability that he left the city in Mercian hands. It was after this alliance that Æthelflæd went to Mercia as a bride.

There is no record of her life at this period, because there was nothing out of the ordinary. Everyone knew what she was and what she had to do: she was a peace-weaver. She had made a political marriage to reward and flatter her father's only effective ally. Her task was to prevent or explain away any misunderstanding between her husband and her kinsmen. Also, she had to keep the powerful Mercian lords, her husband's councillors and war-leaders, in good humour so that they did not turn against Wessex out of ambition, or for Danish bribes, or because they thought they had been insulted. She had to be and to act queenly, in the manner the poets described and her new people expected. The results show that she was a success. The marriage held together; so did the Mercian alliance.[19]

Only one brief comment has survived on record, that shows what she might have thought about her marriage, child-bearing, and the price demanded by her rank. It is intensely interesting, but it was written two centuries after her death.[20] The only way to come near the living woman now is to go after her, to see where she went and what she was doing there.

King Alfred died in 899. King Edward and his brother-in-law went on working smoothly together for the next ten years. Judging from what happened then, they must have spent a lot of the time making ready to take the eastern half of Mercia and the lost kingdom of East Anglia back

---

[19] A queen's duties: *Maxims I*, B 11–20 trans. and edited with introduction and notes in *Poems of Wisdom and Learning in Old English*, T. A. Shippey, Brewer 1976. *Beowulf* ll. 1160–232, 2020–31. The figures of Wealtheow and Freawaru show the stress and danger implied for both of them, under their beauty and gracious manners.

[20] See note 25.

into English hands. However, before the great struggle began, Æthelred's health failed. Later writers say that he had been wounded; perhaps he was left crippled or chronically ill. No word of this has ever been recorded from his lifetime. It would have been prudent for Æthelflæd to make sure that no alarming rumours were spread from her household, to tempt dissidents and encourage the Danes to attack.

In 909, when King Edward began the all-out war against the Danes, and in 910 when he smashed an invasion of Mercia at the battle of Tettenhall, he gave his orders directly to the Mercian forces; they were not being led by Æthelred. And the strengthening of the Mercian defences after Tettenhall was planned and carried out by his wife.

She already knew about fortification: in 907, she and Æthelred had organised the rebuilding and colonisation of the derelict Roman base at Chester. They were giving themselves a port and blocking Norse pirate crews raiding from Ireland. Also, Æthelflæd could try her hand as a *wæpenedmann* and *eorl*, in addition to her wedded duties as *frithuwebbe* and *hlæfdige*. She could take the burden off her husband's shoulders as his strength grew less.

So that when he died in 911, she immediately slipped into his place, ruled the country and commanded the army. There is no hint of objections or counter-claims by anyone else. And no one in England, either churchman or layman, ever said that a woman could not and should not do it.[21] In effect, she was the reigning Queen of Mercia, though she never claimed queenship, for sound personal and political reasons. Her title was 'Lady of the Mercians'.[22]

---

[21] The transference of London, Oxford and the Thames Valley area to Edward's control, so that it became a part of Wessex not Mercia as soon as Æthelred died, has been taken as proof that Edward was ambitious and aggressive, also that he was able to dominate his sister. Edward had the ambition to conquer the Danelaw, with the personality that was needed to succeed. However, London and the lower reaches of the Thames could be much more easily defended from Wessex than from West Mercia. Æthelflæd was faced with the need to defend the Dee and Mersey estuaries and the Welsh border, as well as facing the Danes in Derbyshire and Staffordshire. Edward was doing her a favour by taking her south-east border off her hands.

[22] Æthelflæd held the power and authority of a king of that period and she was born of a royal family. However, it could be embarrassing and potentially dangerous to have another King of Mercia; it could also seem like a provocation to the Mercians to

She can only be known by her acts and decisions. Her movements can be charted in some detail for her last ten years; all but three of the places she chose for her strongholds are known. The shape of her life as Lady of the Mercians can be drawn with lines and dots on a modern map. It is even more revealing to visit these places on the ground or see them from the air, in the same sequence as her history.

During the first five years after Tettenhall, her main effort as war-leader went into keeping watch and ward over Mercia. Wherever she noted a potentially dangerous gap in the defences, she had it fortified to her design. Stenton wrote: "...the fortresses which she built for the protection of Mercia show that she had an eye for country, and the ability to forecast the movements of her enemies." By 915, she had constructed ten strongholds, usually adding two a year, up the Welsh borderland towards the mouths of the Dee and the Mersey, along the 'frontier zone' of the Peak and the East Midlands.[23] This represents a very heavy workload of travelling, supervising and thinking, if she had nothing else to do; but she had the rest of the government to oversee as well.

Æthelflæd's strongholds were not castles, in the later Norman style, parasitic and oppressive on the local land and folk. Following the method devised by her father, she built or restored fortified towns commanding part of the surviving Roman road system. This is one reason why making an 'Æthelflæd Pilgrimage' is such a pleasant and interesting experience now, however toilsome and dangerous her own journeys must have been. These *burhs* were intended in the first place as garrisoned refuges, where the countryfolk could bring their stock in to prevent raiders taking it, and

---

forbid them the use of a royal title once Mercia was re-united. Luckily, the West Saxons had the excuse of their custom to deny the title of 'queen' to their king's wife. It was not a very old custom; there had been queens in early Wessex. Bishop Asser had the story from King Alfred, explaining why the West Saxon dynasty had banned the title. (*Life of Alfred*, ch. 13-15) It is an exciting tale of ambition, murder and sex, with Queen Eadburh cast to play the role of Messalina. West Saxon suspicions were probably roused by memories of her father King Offa rather than of her morals and manners.

[23] The building and fortifying of Æthelflæd's strongholds: 907 Chester (with Lord Æthelred); 910 *Bremesburh* (unidentified) after the battle of Tettenhall(?); 912 *Scergeat* (unidentified), Bridgnorth; 913 Tamworth, Stafford; 914 Eddisbury, Warwick; 915 Chirbury, *Weardburh* (unidentified), Runcorn.

where the local troops could place themselves to strike at the enemy. Yet they were also potential growth-centres for civilised life once peace was restored. Anyone who plots Æthelflæd's moves along the Roman roads can see that everything she did was part of one plan, which she had thought through to the end before she started. And she was not just touring the West Midlands choosing sites for new towns, she was fighting Vikings all the way.

She was also conducting combined operations. While she was holding Mercia, Edward was taking back the east; he could not have done it if she had not been covering his left flank. It is clear that she had placed some of her fortresses – Tamworth, Stafford and Warwick, the ones commanding the east – with a view to seconding his campaigns as well as holding her own ground. They worked together like a right and left hand reaching and gripping further and further to the north.

When the final assault came, that settled the issue between the English and the Danes in the Midlands, she took Derby in 917, after a savage fight. In 918, she advanced on Leicester, but it was surrendered to her without a fight. This was in the Spring; soon afterwards, the Danish Kingdom of York, north of the Humber, sent a formal promise of allegiance to her, not to King Edward.[24] It is possible that a peaceful integration of the north of England at this time – all parties being alarmed by the incursion of the Norsemen from Ireland – might have led to a happier future. In that case, we have reason to be mourning the loss of Æthelflæd to this day.

On the 12th June, she died at Tamworth. The death seems to have taken everyone by surprise. Considering the life she had been leading for the last decade, and that she was elderly by tenth century standards, one guesses that she was working to the last and had driven herself to death.

When we look back at her military record, her years of victorious advances, battles, occupation of territory, we have to ask: what English male commander has ever done better?

But there was something more to Æthelflæd than the ability to control an efficient war-machine. She had only one child, a daughter Ælfwynn. That may have been because either she or Æthelred was infertile, or she

---

[24] Chronicle C (Abingdon), Garmonsway, p.105.

had been injured by miscarriage. But William of Malmesbury, a twelfth century historian who checked his sources, writes that "She was a woman of great soul, who, from the difficulty experienced in her first (or rather only) labour, ever after refused the embraces of her husband, protesting that it was unbecoming the daughter of a king to give way to a delight which in time produced such painful consequences."[25]

Of course, there is a difference between a fact noted down at the time and a story going the rounds two hundred or so years later. However, the stories told about people are part of the evidence about them and about how others reacted to them – provided you don't mix up the different sorts of evidence.

This story is interesting enough as showing a ninth century Englishwoman telling her husband "I have decided that we are not going to have any more children." The reason given is even more interesting, particularly as reported by a medieval churchman in tones of the highest approval. It was not that she thought sex wicked, or that she had decided to vow married chastity as a sacrifice to God: these were good orthodox motives. Æthelflæd said, or was believed to have said, that sexual intercourse was fun while it lasted but that the results were, literally, a bloody nuisance.

However, I believe that Æthelflæd was looking further than her own bodily convenience. Planning ahead was a family characteristic of the House of Wessex. If, as is likely, her daughter Ælfwynn was born fairly early in the marriage, she must have been in her late twenties, perhaps in her thirties when her mother died. By the standards of the time she was well into middle age. It is not reported that any marriage was arranged for her. Yet she did not go into a convent or, a so far as we know, declare a vocation for celibacy. She was not an invalid or half-witted; she

---

[25] The historical writers of the early twelfth century may have had access to many more documents of pre-Norman times than have come down to us. The Normans did not have a policy of destroying Old English material; anything that gave a legal or historical claim was preserved. War, fire, casual accident and the closing of the monasteries in the early sixteenth century caused many more losses. The difficulty of using these writers is that it is impossible to assess lost or unknown sources. They could be lost biographical notes, poems, rumours, popular songs. Also, like Greek and Roman writers, they believed that history was one of the Muses and should be artistically decorated with rhetoric.

witnessed charters. She was not unable or unwilling to take responsibility; she held Mercia after her mother's death until the end of the year. Yet, instead of getting her married and established as heiress of Mercia, Æthelflæd virtually adopted her brother Edward's eldest son, the brilliant Athelstan. According to William of Malmesbury, this arrangement was made by King Alfred himself, so before 899 if the story is true. One can guess why, and also why Æthelflæd made sure that her husband had no son or grandson.

Before the Danish invasions, Mercia and Wessex had been at each other's throats. A newly-independent Mercia, its confidence restored by Æthelflæd's victories, ruled by a son with her ability and the noble memory of the Lord Æthelred, would likely break away from Wessex. It is hard to imagine Edward working in such perfect harmony with a son of Æthelred, once his sister was not there to weave the peace between them. And as soon as English unity frayed and tore, the Vikings would come back through the holes, as they did a century later. It was decided that there would be only one Royal House in England after the reconquest and it would be the House of Cerdic.

Alfred may have planned it, but Æthelflæd made sure it happened, putting the strength of her will on the side of her own family, perhaps even using her own body to bar an independent Mercian dynasty and prepared to sacrifice her own daughter in the same cause. To use the Old English metaphor, Æthelflæd's peace-weaving, her diplomatic marriage, was "of breathtaking brilliance" but it had a lining of tough, hard-wearing ruthlessness.[26]

---

[26] Chronicle C records Æthelflæd's death "twelve days before midsummer" (12th June) in 918. 919 records "In this year too the daughter of Æthelred, Lord of the Mercians, was deprived of all authority in Mercia; she was taken to Wessex three weeks before Christmas. Her name was Ælfwynn." Nothing more is known about her after that. So imagination is free to play around her fate. Edward interrupted his campaign just after the capture of Stamford, and hurried to Tamworth as soon as he heard of Æthelflæd's death. He made sure that all the Mercians who had held rank and office under Æthelflæd had accepted his authority. Then he went back to the east, leaving his niece holding Mercia in her mother's place. When the last two Danish 'capitals' in the east midlands, Nottingham and Lincoln, had surrendered to him, and midwinter had brought fighting to an end, Edward swooped, deprived Ælfwynn of all power and rights in Mercia and removed her into Wessex. Words like 'deprived' and 'taken' suggest injustice and force. The Mercians were not all happy about the West Saxon

Æthelflæd's career was a flesh-and-blood demonstration of how forcefully, as well as how intelligently, women could react to danger. Old English poetry made such female figures vividly alive in the imagination: Hildegyð, Modþryðo, Juliana and Judith are ready to meet insults, threats or attacks with violence; Grendel's mother may be monstrous but she is not presented as ignoble.[27]

These are lively and entertaining passages. However, all the surviving Old English records show that women's place was at peace rather than at war – though 'peace' did not imply sitting quietly and keeping their mouths shut. Naturally, we have more evidence and comment about women of power and wealth; the rich and powerful were the ones who got written about.

Old English literature includes collections of maxims and other Poems of Wisdom and Learning, as Professor Shippey calls them. They are usually known as gnomic or didactic poetry, which makes them sound deadly dull. That is a pity, because they give many vivid little pictures of life as the early English saw it or as they thought it ought to be. One such picture shows a model king and queen:

A king should pay bride-price for a queen with rings and goblets.

(This is the 'gold' that is offered with the formal proposal: the bridegroom is not buying the woman, he is paying for the privilege of her consent and she is the one who takes the price – as in the story of Radigis, confirmed by surviving English marriage contracts.)

---

take-over; some of that resentment may have lingered, to turn people like Eadric Streona against the House of Wessex, as well as personal greed. However, there is no evidence what Ælfwynn thought and felt about the matter. If she and her mother always felt of themselves as heirs of Alfred, and that Edward was closer to them, as blood kin, rather than Æthelred, she may have colluded with her removal and gone happily off to a comfortable nunnery or estate in Wessex.

[27] Hildegyð: *Waldere* ed. F. Norman, Methuen 1933, ll. 1-32.
Modþriðo: *Beowulf* ed. Klaeber, ll. 1931-62.
Juliana: Exeter Book, A.S.P.R. vol. III; ed. Rosemary Woolf, Exeter Medieval Texts 1977, esp. ll. 242-88; 530-58.
Judith: ed. B. J. Timmer (revised ed. 1978).
Grendel's mother: *Beowulf* ll. 1255-95; 1497-1569
Translations of all these passages can be found in *Anglo-Saxon Poetry*: S. A. J. Bradley, Dent 1982.

Both must first and foremost be free with gifts.

(This is because the king must maintain a large and loyal warband, and the royal couple must maintain a good public image.)

The chief must have a warlike spirit; his fighting force must always be increasing. The woman must thrive, loved by her people; she must be light-hearted, absolutely discreet;

(The phrase *rune healdan* means literally "to keep a secret" – a *run* means a 'whisper'; she must not blab what the king tells her in bed. A run is also a symbol of the Old Germanic 'alphabet'; in early times, written letters in any language implied hidden knowledge, ancient wisdom, the 'code'.)

big-hearted in giving horses and treasures. At the ceremonial banquets, she must at all times and places first greet the king in the presence of the assembled retinue, quickly proffer the first cup to her lord's hand. Also she must know what advice to give him, as joint mistress and master of the household together.[28]

What is striking about this particular model is that not only are the king and queen presented as equals in the royal establishment, with the woman having a free hand to dispose of the royal treasure, but that in peacetime she has a more interesting and varied role in the partnership. The king is required to have a fighting spirit that can dominate his nobles and make them confident that he can lead them to victory – he is a *wǽ penmann* – also to provide lavishly for his warriors. She provides the comfort and the charm; she is the mistress of etiquette, the regulator of manners in the great hall, keeping the arrogant and touchy young nobles of the bodyguard from starting quarrels. This is just her public appearance. She is also the king's counsellor and keeper of his secrets; she must be ready at any moment to take her husband's and her kingdom's fate into her hands.

One English queen who swayed her husband by her advice, and who also reverenced the traditional sanctities, was the wife of King Rædwald of East Anglia; he is the most likely owner of the Sutton Hoo treasure now displayed in the British Museum. Bede gives two striking examples of her influence at the beginning of the seventh century.

---

[28] *Maxims* I B ll. 11-22, Poems of Wisdom and Learning: T. A. Shippey; *Women in Anglo-Saxon England*: Christine Fell, pp. 36-7.

Rædwald had been baptized during a visit to Kent. Christianity was new to the English; it was progressive and gave reassuring forecasts about the hereafter. Also, the Bretwalda, Æthelbert of Kent, had opted for it; it provided peaceful links with the wealthy lands to the south. But when Rædwald came home and told the queen what he had done, she persuaded him not to desert the faith of his ancestors. Bede makes it clear that she had a party among the witan to support her. Rædwald was one who liked to keep his options open, so he put a Christian altar in his temple. But the temple remained standing – Rædwald's great-nephew saw it as a boy – and the ancient rites continued for some time.

It would be unfair to expect Bede to approve the queen's piety, or even to mention her name. The only English heathen names he mentions are the ones he needs for his record. Yet in his account of her other decisive intervention, which helped to change the course of English history, his approval is clear. He clothes her words in noble Latin.

North of the Humber, the Anglian kingdoms of Deira (roughly Yorkshire) and Bernicia (Northumberland and Durham; the frontier was around the Tees) were struggling for the mastery. Bernicia had been in the ascendant for a good while; its king Æthelfrith had annexed Deira. The Deiran heir, Edwin, was an exile and Æthelfrith was hunting him from kingdom to kingdom. Finally, about 616, he came to East Anglia and begged for shelter. This was granted; Rædwald promised to protect him. Æthelfrith heard where he was and offered Rædwald a high price to hand him over, or to fix the killing himself to save time and trouble. Rædwald refused at first; but the Northumbrian envoys came a second time, and a third. The price got higher and the threats got worse; finally Rædwald was faced with all-out war. Considering Æthelfrith's record and the forces he could put into the field, Rædwald decided he had no chance of winning. He probably told himself that his first duty was to guard his kingdom. So he sent the envoys back with word that Edwin would either be killed or handed over for killing. A friendly East Anglian warned Edwin that he was already bought and sold, and offered to get him away somewhere that he would never be found. If that was a genuine offer, not a treacherous decoy, the hiding place was probably in the fens. Edwin refused; he had probably had enough of running: let him die where folk could see the murder.

But Bede says that when Rædwald told the queen what he had decided:

She called him back from his purpose, warning him that no reason can justify a great king in selling his best friend, in his hour of need, for gold – and even worse, losing his honour, most precious of treasures, for love of money. What need to say more? The king did as she said.

Bede was writing over a century after the event, working up her speech in his elegant phrases from some report in his sources. Translated into Old English verse, they could be fitted into *Beowulf* or *The Battle of Maldon* without sounding out of place. So far as I know, they are the first words attributed to an Englishwoman in an English historical document.[29]

Once the queen had made up his mind for him, Rædwald moved fast. As soon as the Northumbrian envoys had gone home, he rushed his army towards the Deiran frontier. Æthelfrith had to meet him before he had gathered his whole force. The battle was fought in the Mercian borderland on the east bank of the River Idle; Æthelfrith was defeated and killed. So Edwin became king of the two northern kingdoms and presided over the start of the great Northumbrian cultural renaissance. Rædwald became the next *bretwalda*, which possibly helps to explain the richness of the Sutton Hoo treasure. So the queen's advice had been very profitable for both of them. She lost her eldest son in the battle, but we have her word for it that honour is not cheap.

According to the Maxim of queenship, one of the essential qualities of the ideal queen – she who must be counsellor, hostess, peace-weaver – is that she must be *leohtmod*. The word means 'light-hearted, cheerful'; it can also mean frivolous. If queens are depressed, nervous, bad-tempered and are seen to be, they are obviously expecting the disasters they are trying to dispel. Yet it could not have been easy for Rædwald's queen to pretend to be light-hearted while she was waiting for messengers from the River Idle. The Northumbrian army might be bringing the news. The early English were well aware that the bejewelled woman walking round the mead hall, gracious and smiling, with just the right words of greeting

---

[29] Rædwald's queen: her defence of her religion: Bede, *Historia Ecclesiastica Gentis Anglorum* Book II ch. 15 para. 1; her defence of Edwin and of her king's honour ibid. ch. 12.

for the king's champions and his guests, could be carrying a terrible burden of responsibility and fear.

Such a moment, when only a queen's self-control and poise carries her company out of immediate danger, is brilliantly dramatised in *Beowulf*.[30] The great victory feast has as many perilous undercurrents as a dinner party in a Jane Austen novel. On the surface it is a happy celebration: the monster Grendel is dead at last, so the royal court is free of the terror and death that stalked it so long. But Grendel was killed by a young foreigner, who had succeeded in one night after the Danish champions had failed for years; this cannot be unmixed joy for them.

However, in the excited atmosphere, someone has started the rumour, which is sweeping the court, that King Hrothgar means to adopt Beowulf as his son. This would make him a rival to the king's own two sons, who are still young and untried warriors. Also, still more alarming, he would be a rival to the king's powerful and dangerous nephew, Hrothulf, who is the second man in the kingdom and is now sitting beside the king in the place of honour. One careless word or action and all hell could be let loose.

This is the moment, described in *Maxims*, when Queen Wealtheow steps forward to present the first cup to the king and speak the ceremonial words of greeting. She has got problems. She has got to scotch the rumour about the adoption, publicly, but without insulting Beowulf – after all, he has just saved the royal palace and the feast is in his honour. Also, she has to show Hrothulf, and the Danish war-band and nobles, how ungrateful and shameful it would be if he turned on her boys and murdered them after the king's death, as well he might. She has to indicate to Hrothulf that if he does try to get rid of her sons, she could set Beowulf on him, as she is making a big play for Beowulf's gratitude and friendship even though she does not want him as an adopted son. And she cannot say anything of this openly.

---

[30] *Beowulf* ll.1008-67; 1159-233. The rejoicings begin at line 1008 when the king enters the great hall, and the account of the ceremonies continues to the moment when the royal *scop* begins to recite. There is a pause while the company listens to a story which ends with a Danish queen being taken back to her country in triumph by Danish warriors – leaving her husband, her son and her brother dead by violence. It is after that (l.1159) that Wealtheow comes forward to make her speech, well aware what danger lies behind friendly meetings.

One would think it was impossible, but the poem shows her doing it beautifully. One can imagine her smiling all the time, though she must have been terrified. Professor Shippey writes of this passage:

She is striving to evoke the *dream* (joy) for which she so desperately wishes. All spells proceed from the belief that if you say something the right way, it will come true and that is what she is doing.

The queen is not just practising diplomacy and counselling, she is practising magic.

Rædwald's queen was a devout follower of the old religion. This faith had always set a high value on women as counsellors, because as a sex they were believed to have special psychic powers. Tacitus wrote "...they believe that there is something innately holy and prophetic in women";[31] as a result, men consult them and respect their advice. Some names of these holy women have been preserved in Latin records: the mysterious Albruna, who was already a memory of ancient times when Tacitus was writing at the end of the first century; Veleda, who was treated as a divinity by the west German tribes in Vespasian's reign, guiding the Rhineland revolt from her high tower by the River Lippe; Ganna, who was Veleda's successor, received with honour by the Emperor Domitian when she came to Rome on a state visit; Gambara, the Langobard matriarch and personal friend of the goddess Frija.

Written English history is Christian history. It begins with Bede, who was composing a history of the English Church. So though he mentions political queens, including a pagan political queen, we do not read about any priestesses and prophetesses of the old religion. What we do find in Bede's book – what we find right through early English life, in writings of various kinds: history, biography, personal letters, legal documents – are glimpses of immensely powerful holy women of the new religion.

---

[31] Tacitus: *Germania* ch. 8.
Dictionary of Northern Mythology: entries under Albruna, Gambara, Ganna, Seeresses, Veleda, with references; details from Latin and Greek writers can be checked in the Loeb Classical Library volumes, with parallel English translations
History of the Lombards: Paul the Deacon trans. W. D. Foulke, Univ. Pennsylvania Press 1974.

These were the abbesses, usually of royal blood, who ruled the great double monasteries of women and men. Most people have at least heard of Hild, Abbess of *Streanœshalch* (Whitby) because she fostered the talent and poetic innovations of Cædmon, who was one of her estate workers. In fact, she made her House the university college of the north. Bede uses words that echo what Tacitus said of Veleda six hundred years earlier: "Kings and great noblemen used to seek her counsel".[32]

Less well known to the general public is her younger cousin Ælfflæd, whom she brought up and who succeeded her as Abbess. Like Hild, she had intelligence, skill and tact. She was certainly a brilliant peace-weaver: in 706, she even managed to settle a dispute that had been raging since 678, between the princely and formidable bishop Wilfrid on the one side and the successive kings of Northumbria on the other – this quarrel had baffled the Archbishop of Canterbury and the Pope, and managed to involve Mercia, the Frankish government and the king of the Frisians, to name but a few. So Ælfflæd certainly performed a miracle in 706.

Her greatest service to her people had been given in 695. Her brother, King Ecgfrith, had led his army north into Pictland, where he and they had been wiped out by the Picts at the battle of *Nechtansmere*. He had no direct male heir, but there were enough noble families with some royal blood from the two Northumbrian dynasties to start a free-for-all civil war; meanwhile the Picts, the Mercians and the Strathclyde Welsh were waiting across the frontiers to come raiding in.

Now, just before Ecgfrith set out on his march north, long before any word of disaster, Ælfflæd sent an urgent message to Cuthbert, the saintly and charismatic hermit of Lindisfarne. He found her distressed; she had a foreknowledge of the disaster in Pictland. She wanted to sound Cuthbert out about an unknown half-brother, Aldfrith. He was the son of a liaison between King Oswiu and an Irishwoman; he had wisely been keeping well away from Northumbria and was studying in Iona. Cuthbert

---

[32] Abbess Hild:– Bede, H.E.G.A. Bk. IV ch.23.

The entry in *A Biographical Dictionary of Dark Age Britain* is brief but useful, as it gives cross references to her connections. A. Williams, A. P. Smyth, D. P. Kirby, Seaby 1991

The Coming of Christianity to Anglo-Saxon England: ch. 10. The Northumbrian Monasteries, esp. pp. 149-52: Whitby: H. Meyr-Harting, Battsford 1991 (3rd ed.).

approved her choice; so when news of the disaster arrived, Ælfflæd had her nomination ready. The power and respect of her character and position made Aldfrith's accession go smoothly. He proved an excellent and successful ruler.[33]

In the contemporary biography of Wilfred. Ælfflæd is described as "the comforter and best counsellor of the whole province." One might think that there was nothing in common between Christian nuns in seventh and eighth century England and these pagan Germanic women of the first century that Tacitus mentioned. Yet these royal and high-born abbesses were also holy women. They lived apart, like Veleda in her tower, but kings and nobles sought their counsel – and followed it; their advice helped to decide the actions and fate of their kingdoms. They too had extra-sensory powers; when invoked they could perform supernatural actions, though they usually waited till after death to do so.[34]

"The women must be light-hearted." *Leohtmod* can be interpreted as 'cheerful' or as 'lightminded, frivolous'. The queens and abbesses of early English fact, as well as the famous heroines of early English legend, were expected to be gracious to their nobles and guests, to hide fear and stress. The abbesses, at any rate, attained serenity. But none of them is shown in a mood of light-hearted pleasure. They all had to bear a heavy weight of responsibility; also, they had their dignity to preserve.

Certainly, there were accusations of frivolity, usually made by bishops; there were abbesses and nuns who spent time and money on fine

---

[33] Abbess Ælfflæd:– *Dictionary of Dark Age Britain* pp. 5-6.
Bede: *H.E.G.A.* Bk. III ch. 24: Dedicated to God by her father's vow; trained by Hild.
Bede: *Life of St. Cuthbert* gives the story of Ælfflæd and the Northumbrian succession; Eddius Stephanus (Eddi) gives the story of her peace-making at the River Nidd, in his *Life of St. Wilfrid*. Both lives have been translated by J. A. Webb, with an introduction and bibliography by D. H. Farmer in *The Age of Bede* Penguin Books 1988. See pp. 72-75 for Ælfflæd and Cuthbert; pp. 171-74 for Ælfflæd and Wilfrid. Both lives and the introduction repay study.

[34] The women saints of England make an interesting subject of study for people interested in local history, place-names and Church dedications, attitudes to women and also folk-lore. Some are still well known: Hild, Etheldreda (*Æthelryth*) of Ely, Werburga (*Wærburh*) of Chester, Mildred (*Mildreth*) of Thanet. St. Frideswide of Oxford, patroness of the University, is the heroine of a romantic story. St. Uncumber seems to be the patroness of wishful thinking.

clothes, hair-dressing and manicure. There are hints of lively scandals: for example, the goings-on in the monastery at Coldingham[35] and the continental career of Queen Eadburh.[36]

The advice given to aristocratic lay-women by the *maxims* is:– not to refuse love affairs before marriage, just to be very careful about organising them.

"A lady, a virgin, must visit her lover by stealth, if she does not want to achieve a public and formal proposal of marriage."[37]

Note that the high-born maiden does not sit in her bower hoping that her lover may climb in at midnight; she goes to hunt him out – *hire freond gesecan*.

One wonders why a lady should be <u>unwilling</u> to receive a tempting proposal, complete with bride-price and a morning-gift to come, that would make her the delight of her kin, the envy and honour of her shire. The advice is ironic. Of course, any sensible woman would look forward to a good establishment. A sure way to wreck one's chances was to try to carry on a secret love affair at the same time – there would always be someone who knew and told. This short sentence in *Maxims II* contains the main plot of every Restoration comedy; it is interesting that the Old English words already carry the same tone of ironic amusement.

Though this passage shows a woman of that society doing what she chooses, she is still constrained to be furtive and cunning if she is to avoid the damage of ruin.

"A roving woman causes talk – *widgongel wif word gespringeð* – folk often slander her and smirch her name."

Rumour-mongering could be as vicious then as it is today. At least this warning shows that women in early England were no more housebound by law and custom than the Wife of Bath and her cronies; also that there was a society where women could roam around and get talked about. It is admitted that rumour could be unjust.

There is a description of a woman enjoying frank and untroubled happiness, not caring who knows it. She is not a lady of rank. Her

---

[35] Bede: *H.E.G.A.* Bk. IV ch. 25.

[36] Asser: *Life of Alfred* ch. 13-15.

[37] *Maxims II*, ll. 44-46, *Poem of Wisdom and Learning* pp. 78-79.

husband has a hard and dangerous job; she is thankful to afford food and clothes. This happy woman is the wife of a Frisian merchant-seaman and she loves him. His ship has come in; she is on top of the world when she knows that it has been safely beached and "her man is home, her own bread-winner." She calls him in, strips off his filthy salt-caked clothes to wash, gets him a fresh shirt and "gives him on land what his love needs."[38] It sounds as if they spend the first day in bed.

The same note of honest enjoyment is heard in some of the riddles of the Exeter Book anthology. The *Riddles*[39] are not a collection of bawdy jokes; nor are they brain-teasers in the Christmas cracker or puzzle-book sense of the word. They are clever, often very lovely, animistic poems about the strange lives of other creatures. These are described in terms that are true but deliberately misleading. The bawdy ones work in the same way as the scripts of 'Carry-On' films. Something completely neutral – putting a key in a lock, proving dough, working a churn – is worded in a way that invites the hearers to imagine sexual activity. Then they are challenged to name the subject. Anyone who falls into the trap can be jeered at, as having a mind that can only think of one thing.

Like the 'Carry-On' films, the Old English riddles contain nothing vicious or sadistic; there is no gloating over the use of sex as a means of humiliation or degradation. The feeling is cheerful, hearty relish, like enjoying a good meal or a lively game. Like the Frisian sailor's wife, the roving women taking part in these bouts are not passive objects – anything but.

For example, in Riddle 25, there is a description which is officially of a farmer's lovely daughter pulling up onions from the onion bed, shutting them up tight in her store-room, and finding her eyes water when she makes use of them. Whatever it is that is shaggy down below, stands erect and grows tall in a bed, it is the girl who does the grabbing.

Even more striking is Riddle 91. This has been interpreted as a key going into a keyhole; as such, some of its phrases are difficult to explain.

---

[38] *Maxims* IB ll. 24-29.

[39] *The Exeter Book* (pp.180–210; 229–43): Krapp & Dobbie, Columbia U.P./Routledge & Kegan Paul 1936. *The Exeter Riddle Book*: trans. and introduced by Kevin Crossley-Holland, drawings by Virgil Burnett, Folio Society 1978.

Edith Williams has pointed out that the action is being related by the keyhole, not the key; its inner lock is working in enthusiastic collaboration (*ascufan* and *bregdan* – shoving and vibrating – are two of the verbs) as the key is thrust in so that the lord can get to his treasure:

"Often I open wide to that which pricks against me, when, wound with rings, I press firmly against a hard one; pierced from the rear, I push for what my lord hopes to get at midnight."

The main idea given by these poems is that when sex was not being complicated by passion, longing, despair or blood-feuding, the early English took it as friendly good-humoured fun for both sexes.

But life, particularly sexual life, generally does not stay uncomplicated for long. There is a short poem in the Exeter Book, placed just in front of the first riddle. It is now usually known as *Wulf and Eadwacer*. Its language is simple; at least, the words that were used to make it are simple. What baffles its readers more than all the 95 riddles, is that everyone who reads it and then compares notes with other readers, seems to have read a different message in it – or into it. It is not so much a riddle as a spell in the Modern as well as the Old English sense of the word.[40]

The poem is spoken as by a woman; it could have been written by a woman. We know the names and some of the works of Englishwomen in this period who wrote and taught in Latin; anyone who can compose verse in Latin can compose in English. But if these lines were written by a man, they are even more remarkable. He must have been one of those rare ones, like Shakespeare or Richardson, who can really imagine what it is like to be a woman.

---

[40] (a) Some idea of the effect that reading *Wulf and Eadwacer* in the original O.E. can have on the reader, can be got by looking at a critical study and its references. *Wulf and Eadwacer: A woman's cri de coeur – for whom, for what?*, Henk Aertsen; in *Companion to Old English Poetry* edited by H. Aertsen and R. H. Bremmer Jr. VU Univ. Press, Amsterdam 1994. This essay gives an account of earlier interpretations of the lyric.

(b) A 'spell' in M. English is defined as: 1. a word or formula used to work magic; 2. compelling attraction, fascination; a bewitched state, a trance.
A *spel* or *spell* in O.E. was 1. a story, a narrative; 2. an instructive talk, discourse, sermon; 3. a message; 4. a false or foolish story, an 'old wives' tale'.

The woman in this poem is emotionally and sexually bound to two men at once. Eadwacer may be her husband, or her abductor. At any rate, he is the man-in-residence; the name may be her bitter nickname for him, as it means 'watchman of property'. Wulf is the man she wants; he may be an outlaw (a wolf's head); a member of a hostile tribe or a bloodfeuding kin-group; he may be a sailor who can only visit her at brief intervals. They both have homes on islands in the fens, so when it has been raining for a long time and the waters rise, he cannot get to her at all.

Modern readers can study the clues provided in the poem and construct their own plot. Perhaps the first listeners and readers did so too. Or perhaps there was some old tale or contemporary disaster that could be recognised at once by some detail or allusion.

What the poem leaves in no doubt at all is the woman's gut-aching hunger for Wulf; she says it makes her bodily sick, it feels like starving to death. The weather that keeps Wulf away keeps Eadwacer at home; he passes the time making love to her. As she is sitting crying, he may even assume that he is comforting her. With extraordinary honesty with herself, she admits that though she hates his love-making (because he is the wrong man), she is enjoying it at the same time (presumably because it satisfies her physical desire).

"That was a delight to me," she says, "yet I loathed it too."

The Old English makes her mean it in the sound of the words and their feel in the mouth, as well as in the choice of vocabulary: "*wæs me win to þon*" is a caress, putting the lips and mouth ready for a kiss; "*wæs me hwæþre eac lað*" ends in a spit and a snarl.

This woman has a child. The poem does not state whose it is, but it is clear that she is planning to hand it over to Wulf, and to tell Eadwacer that 'a wolf' got it and carried it off to the woods. Whether the baby is Eadwacer's, or he only thinks it is, she knows that this act of hers will mark the destruction of their union – if there was anything to destroy. The last two lines of the poem give her mind-bending comment: "It is easy for anyone to tear apart something that was never joined – the song of us two together."

"Us two" are herself and Eadwacer. In this moment of total rejection, the poet makes a beautiful metaphor of real marriage: a song for two voices that have to be equally balanced. This woman and Eadwacer never had a song. Yet the phrase is a recognition, like her admission that she got pleasure from his love-making, that they could have had one.

When a situation like this was again explored in depth in English literature – by a woman, in *Wuthering Heights* – there was a reaction of shock and distaste that women could be imagined to have such feelings. By contrast *Wulf and Eadwacer*, whenever it had previously been composed, was chosen to make part of an expensive eleventh century anthology, that was owned and presented to his cathedral by Leofric, the first bishop of Exeter. The poem was socially acceptable.

It has been suggested that the poem was based on one of the passionate and tragic episodes in the heroic legends – like the terrible mating of Sigemund and his sister – which had no resemblance to the events and moral code of English life centuries after the Conversion. It could be enjoyed as an entertainment, an exercise of imagination.

However, there is the same open-mindedness about women in the *Maxims*, which are presented as life-as-it-is. The description of the Frisian seaman's wife welcoming her husband is reasonably well-known to the general reader, because it has been quoted in modern books about early English life. The lines that follow are hardly ever quoted. Yet they deserve to be studied by everyone who thinks about the early English attitude to women because they are not intended to be striking or provocative, merely statements of an obvious truth.[41]

This comment about women – sailors' women, women whose men have to go away – could have been written in this century, during the second World War. As women are referred to as 'they', it is supposed to be spoken by a man; it is non-judgmental and compassionate:

"A woman should keep a contract with a man. Folk often defame them and blacken their characters. Many of them are steadfast; many are inquisitive, they make love with foreign men when their husband goes far away. A seaman will be away for a long time; however one should always look and hope for one's lover, wait for what cannot be hurried. When he gets a good opportunity, he will

---

[41] *Maxims* 1B ll. 30-37.

come home, if he is alive and well, unless the sea removes him, the ocean has the war-ship in its clutches."

Note that the opposite to 'steadfast', 'faithful' is not 'unfaithful', 'treacherous' but 'inquisitive', 'curious'. The Maxim accepts the fact that a woman may go with a strange man, not because she is wild with desire or desperation, but just interested to find out how he performs. There is a realisation, too, of what it is to be lonely, with no means of knowing when a man will come back or if he will ever come back. There is no easy optimism; the male persona can only advise waiting, because if a man loves his woman he will come home to her when he can – if he has not been drowned. Faithfulness is a counsel of perfection but it is recognised that some women find the dreary waiting unbearable. And then there is the new arrival – the Danish trader, the allied serviceman.

However, both Old English imaginative literature and early English historical fact show that not all women were prepared to sit gazing hopefully out to sea, whether they were waiting for a lover's return or scanning the horizon for a replacement. The first surviving account of an Englishwoman, in the middle of the sixth century, shows her taking ship to confront her betrothed husband.

In another Exeter Book poem, now called *The Husband's Message*,[42] a piece of wood carved with runes gives a message to a woman from a man who had exchanged vows with her. He had been driven into exile by a feud; now at last he has a home that he thinks fit to offer a noble and beautiful lady. He has his own hall and a splendid band of loyal followers, he is living like a king – he may even be a king, if this poem is based on traditions of the migration. And none of it will mean anything without her; she alone is the meaning and value of his life. The carved stick is supposed to be speaking; in other words, she looks at the token and "gets the message".

[42] *The Husband's Message*: A.S.P.R. Vol. III pp. 225-27:
ed. in *Three Old English Elegies*, with introduction, notes and glossary by R. F. Leslie Univ. of Essex 1988;
with introduction and parallel verse trans. in *A Choice of Anglo-Saxon Verse*, Richard Hamer Faber and Faber 1970.

"Now this man has overcome his troubles; he lacks no desirable thing: horses, precious objects, joys of the hall or any noble treasure in the world, O prince's daughter, if he may have you."

In realistic terms, a foot-loose man who had won power and wealth in a foreign country could get a rich and influential wife there, with no questions asked before the growth of international law and international communications. However, he only wants her, and without her all his gains will be destitution.

This declaration sounds very courtly and romantic – but these words 'courtly' and 'romantic' sound oddly out of place when they are used of an English poem that was composed at any time before the early eleventh century, possibly a long time before. They seem to belong to some Provencal lyric or to a French tale of chivalry. Romance was evolved in the Latin-based languages of the old Gaulish provinces; it was imported into England in the twelfth century.

Certainly, the Old English poem is different from courtly romance in one important feature. The medieval knight goes off to kill his dragon or confront the evil sorcerer, while his lady sits in her tower till he comes back in triumph to claim her. The English husband asks his lady, very politely, to take ship and make her way overseas to join him, as soon as spring weather makes voyages possible.

The feud must still be raging; he cannot come back to get her, or even communicate with her except by a coded message in runes. She can hardly tell her royal father that she is setting off to join the exile and make a public departure. Yet if she is living at the centre of a royal household, it will be almost impossible to leave secretly – how is she going to get her luggage and her servants away? If she goes alone, a desirable woman with jewels and other valuables, she will be asking for trouble. Will she disguise herself as a boy, like Shakespeare's Imogen in a similar situation? When she gets to the coast, she will have to charter a ship, or take a passage in one, and trust that the shipman is honest, not a pirate or slave-dealer. If the shipman is honest, there is always the chance that his ship will be taken by pirates or wrecked. And if she reaches the foreign land, what will she do then? What language do the folk talk there? Will she know where to go to find her man?

Her devoted lover says not a word of anxiety or apology for all these problems and dangers he is leaving her to cope with. He just tells her: "Don't let any living man deter you from travelling or prevent you from making the journey." This is not because he is making light of the woman, whistling her to him as if she were an obedient dog – the whole tone of the poem is as worshipful as an Elizabethan sonnet. It is because in his eyes, as well as being the world's greatest treasure, she is also a perfectly competent human adult. She can make the same journey as he did, without needing her hand held, or someone else to do the thinking for her.

The poem gives no suggestion or clue whether she arrived.

One may object: this is poetry read for pastime, creating an imaginary world and probably based on some tale from the migration. If the poem's first listeners wondered about the heroine's fate, or argued whether a woman could or should make such a journey, what were the answers they could find in their contemporary society?

About 725, the Abbess Hæaburg, whose short name was Bucge, felt in need of spiritual refreshment from the cares of administering a double monastery. She wanted to make a pilgrimage to Rome. She wrote to ask for advice from the Devon man Winfrith, (St. Boniface, Apostle of Germany) as being resident in Europe and having visited Rome more than once. He wrote back:

"This is what our sister Wihtburg did. She has told me by letter that she has found at the shrine of St. Peter the kind of quiet life she had long sought for in vain. After I had written to her about your intentions, she sent me word that you would do better to wait until the attacks and threats of the Saracens against Rome had died down and until she herself could send you an invitation. To me also, this seems the better plan. Make all the necessary plans for the journey, wait for word from her, and after that, do whatever God's grace shall inspire you to do."

One has to admire the unflappable English calm of "our sister Wihtburg", finding the kind of quiet life she had long sought, while hordes of fanatical Moslem warriors ravaged the Italian countryside and rampaged round the walls of Rome. Also admirable is the response of Boniface, the celibate male cleric. He did not tell the Abbess that her plan was too dangerous, unfeminine, that she would do better to stay at home and stitch an altar cloth. He referred her to a woman's opinion – a woman who had already made the trip – told her to consider Wihtburg's advice and then make up her own mind. Notice that he takes it for granted God inspires women and talks to them directly without need for a male priest as interpreter. The fact that he suggests the Abbess should start packing at once shows that he guessed what Wihtburg's advice would be and approved of it.

Yet "the attacks and threats of the Saracens" were a terrifying prospect. A few years later, Charles Martel's victory at Poitiers in 732 halted their northwards invasion of France, but the danger did not go away at once, not for centuries. Yet Boniface seems as unworried as the lover in the poem at the thought that Hæaburg could be going to her death, or to what used to be called "a fate worse than death". In fact, she reached Rome in safety, returned in safety and took up the rule of her double monastery again. Other women did not return. Some died on the way, not just by violence but from sickness and exhaustion; it was a gruelling journey. In 667, an English Archbishop-elect, arriving in Rome to be consecrated and receive his pallium – and presumable travelling with every comfort and attention – died there. Bishop Ceolfrid, setting out from Northumbria in 716 with the superb bible, now known as the Codex Amiatinus, as a gift for the Pope did not arrive: he died in France. Some women set out as pilgrims but stayed on as prostitutes. There was an exciting context of overseas adventure for reading *The Husband's Message*.

Abbess Hæaburg set out to brave the Saracens and all the other perils during the great missions to Frisia and Germany led by Willibrord (658-739) and Boniface (675-755).[43] The English had never forgotten

---

[43] The Frisian and German Missions.

Anglo-Saxon England ch. V The English Church from Theodore to Boniface pp.165-76, F. M. Stenton. O.U.P. 1971.

The Missionaries and some of their friends and helpers can be found in *Dictionary of Dark Age Britain*.

The background of the period: *England and the Continent in the Eighth Century*: W. Levison, Oxford 1946.

Scholarship of the period: *The Coming of Christianity to Anglo-Saxon England* ch. 12 Books and Studies. Note especially the influence of Aldhelm.

their roots in their former homelands, as is shown by their continuing love of the old heroic legends. They were concerned about the spiritual fate of their Germanic kinsfolk and wanted to share good news – *god-spell* – with them. In 738, Boniface sent a letter addressed to all English, calling them to pray for the continental Saxons: "we are of one and the same blood and bone".[44] There is nothing quite like these missions in the history of the western church. The missionaries were not individual enthusiasts. The mission had nationwide backing, yet there was no prospect of military conquest, political power or loot for any English king. Perhaps that is one reason why so little is recorded about it in later English history; most of the documents and artefacts are on the continent.

The venture was also different from any other missionary enterprise of the convert churches in the official share that women took in it. This was not just collecting for the missionaries, keeping up a stream of encouraging letters, carrying out commissions like copying luxury manuscripts or sending parcels of comforts from England, though women did all that as well. The male missionaries asked the women to come out and work with them; they needed the woman's special contribution to complete the job.

The German lands beyond the old Rhine-Danube frontier were awesome. Tacitus has given a vivid picture of hardened Roman soldiers beginning to lose their nerve as they made their way into the eerie Teutoberger Wald, especially when they came upon the remains of three legions that had been massacred there six years before – and the nearby sacred groves where their officers had been sacrificed.[45]

Women missionaries and scholars: *Women in Anglo-Saxon England* ch. 6 The Religious Life.

Letters to and from the continental missions: *The Letters of St. Boniface* E. Emerton New York 1973; *The Anglo-Saxon Missionaries on the Continent* C. H. Talbot, Sheed and Ward 1954.

The Life of St. Leoba ibid.

The letters of Berhtgyð have been translated and discussed in *Women Writers of the Middle Ages* pp. 30-35, Peter Dronke, C.U.P. 1984.

[44] Boniface: letter 46. Quoted in *The Coming of Christianity* ch. 15 St. Boniface: Mirror of English History p. 264 and note.

[45] Tacitus: Annals Bk. I ch. 60 para. 2 "He himself, with few legions (*ipse inpositas navibus quattuos legiones*) –" to end of ch. 62. It is still chilling to read.

Boniface was hacked to death. The women who crossed the sea to Germany and worked there successfully for the rest of their lives are proved, by the very fact of doing so, to have been brave, tough and competent. Enough of their writings remain to show that they were also literate, scholarly and creative. They should be better remembered in their native land.

For example, St. Walburh trained at Wimborne in Dorset, then went with her two brothers to join the German mission. She became abbess of the double monastery of Heidensheim, which had a distinguished scholarly record. Her feast day is May 1st, so in her district the rites of Spring become traditionally celebrated as *Walpurgisnacht*. This is not a sarcastic joke but a tribute to her power, ranking her locally with such mighty ones as St. Michael and St. John the Baptist.

Huneberc of Heidenheim was one of her nuns. (C. Fell reads the name as '*Hugeburc*', that is *Hygeburg*). She wrote the first surviving English travel book, the *Hodoeporicon of St. Willibald*, based on the account he gave her of his travels and adventures during his pilgrimage to the Holy Land. Her choice of title shows that she, like so many English nuns, had read and studied the brilliant but fiendishly difficult works of St. Aldhelm of Sherbourne.

Berhtgit (Berhtgyð) went out with her mother Chunihilt (Cynehild); they were appointed as teachers in the region of Thuringia. The Germanic author of a *Life of Boniface* describes the two women as "very learned in the liberal arts". These were the studies preserved from the old Classical education, which the Catholic Church had inherited from the Roman Empire. This education had now been put to the service of Christian theology – the study of sacred scripture and commentary – but it also demanded ability to read and write Latin, knowledge of history, astronomical and mathematical calculations to work out the correct time of Easter and other dates, and a command of classical metres and rhetorical techniques. The works of Bede, Aldhelm and Alcuin show the quality of English scholarship in the seventh and eighth centuries. The learned abbesses of the English double monasteries, and their pupils who taught and presided in the new German foundations, were, in modern terms, holding M.A. degrees.

Berhtgit outlived her kin and learned the full meaning of loneliness. Yet her letters are not spontaneous moans and yelps of pain – they would not have been preserved and copied if they had been – they are conscious works of literary art. This does not mean that they are insincere, any more than Milton's Lycidas is an insincere expression of bereavement. The literary skill is part of the writer's intellectual truth.

One of the most gifted of the women in this group was Leofgyth, known and canonised by her pet name 'Leoba' – Darling. She was a young kinswoman of Boniface on the mother's side. She had an early taste for writing Latin verses – in fact, she first introduced herself to him with a request that he would be what today would be called her pen-friend, by sending him one of her first efforts to correct. By 749, when he sent for her to help him, she was mistress (scholastica) of the younger nuns in the double monastery at Wimborne. Her abbess felt her departure as a serious loss. She led a party of thirty nuns to Germany; Boniface installed them at Tauberbischofsheim in Franconia, with Leoba as abbess. We have to think of Somerville and Girton in the early years of this century to get a sense of the atmosphere. Leoba's influence spread outside church circles: as well as bishops, lay governors – princes and nobles – asked her advice. She was invited to the Carolingian court: Charlemagne's wife Hildegarde loved and admired her.

In 754, when he was about 79, Boniface resigned his archbishopric on account of his age. He decided to spend his retirement working in Frisia, the most warlike and dangerous of the mission fields. Even if he had stayed in the peace of his favourite monastery at Fulda, it is unlikely that his life would have lasted much longer, but he seems to have had some presentiment of his sudden and bloody end, because he left instructions about what should be done after his death.

He wanted his body brought back to Fulda for burial. And he begged Leoba to promise him to stay on in Germany after his death. Perhaps she, like Berhtgit, had been feeling homesick; perhaps she had imagined how alien Germany would feel for her when Boniface was no longer there. So in his will he required two amazing concessions for her: that she should be admitted into the monastery when she wanted, to pray by his tomb; and that when she died, she should be buried with him. These are his words:

"that her bones should be placed next to him in the tomb, so that they who had served God with equal sincerity and zeal should await together the day of resurrection".

There is no doubt that they loved each other. The fact that he wanted her body to lie beside him till they woke again shows that he felt a personal love for her as a particular woman, not just a remote link to a fellow spirit. This is a rare kind of love between men and women, that one does not often expect to meet before the nineteenth century. It is still not very common today: the deep emotional comradeship that comes from shared work and temperamental affinity between equals.

Leoba was faithful to his last request; she stayed in Germany until her death twenty-eight years later. She was buried at Fulda – but not in his grave. The monks could not bring themselves to go that far.

There have always been daring and independent-minded women in all races and all centuries, who have achieved brilliant results. But so far as I know, after the Norman invasion, there were no other 'Establishment' invitations to groups of Englishwomen for help and co-operation; nor any officially-recognised enterprise by a group of Englishwomen overseas till Florence Nightingale took her nurses to the Crimea.

We know so much about the women of the German mission, because they were literate and vowed to religion. That meant they wrote in Latin, so that their writings could be read and appreciated across Latin Christendom, therefore copies were made. Also, they were holy women, so their writings were preserved in monastic archives, where they were relatively safe as the centuries passed.

We know practically nothing, except what poetry tells us, about the thoughts and feelings of English laywomen in this early part of our history. Apart from short inscriptions in runic letters, there is hardly any writing outside monasteries, and very little 'private' writing – personal letters – even there. The reason we have so many letters to and from the German missionaries is just because they were abroad and could not visit or send verbal messages very easily. As for the existence of individual layfolk, a name engraved on a ring or brooch, a curt statement in a legal document, is usually all we have.

Certainly. it can be said that numbers of early Englishwomen wrote their names on the map of England.[46] One of the most common forms of early English place-names is the definition of a natural feature, or an establishment – grove, clearing, dairy-farm, etc. – with a personal name in the possessive form. The name may give the owner or founder of a place, or perhaps they were connected with it by some exploit, like the later Nan Clark's Lane, in Mill Hill, said to be so-called because she was murdered in it and haunts it.

A considerable proportion of personal names in these Old English constructions is feminine. For example, the word for a clearing or meadow was *leah* (Modern English lea). Kimberley in Norfolk was Cyneburg's clearing. One might please to imagine her, axe in hand like an American pioneer woman, marking off her territory but most likely she just owned it.

Significant of women's independence are the names that mean property, especially landed property. A *ham* is a dwelling; Babraham in Cambridgeshire was Beaduburh's *ham*. A *tun* is enclosed land around a dwelling; later, it could mean an estate with a village community, a manor: Wollaton in Shropshire was Wulfwynn's *tun*. A larger type of property is a *worth* or *worthig*: an enclosed homestead with surrounding lands. These could be estates of great extent and importance; the suffix is often used of royal estates. Kenilworth in Warwickshire was Cynehild's *worth*.

Most interesting of all, because it denotes power as well as wealth, is *burh*, *burg*. A 'bury' or borough was originally a fortress. In one instance, Bamburgh, we know from Bede that a royal stronghold of the Bernicians was named after an early Bernician queen: it was *Bebbanburh*, Bebbe's fortress. In other examples, the suffix could mean the precinct walls round a monastic establishment. There is a chain of thought: early Christian kings gave derelict Roman forts, particularly on the coast, to missionary priests. From this use, the name was extended to other buildings that were walled away from worldly life and use: Peterborough only became a 'borough' when St. Peter's minster was built there; before that, the place was called *Medeshamstede*. The

---

[46] *The Historical Bearing of Place-Name Studies: The Place of Women in Anglo-Saxon Society* F. M. Stenton Transactions of the Royal Historical Society, Fourth Series, vol. 25 pp. 1-13. Then hunt through the Place-names of chosen counties.

abbesses of the great double monasteries held wide estates as well as political influence. Tetbury in Gloucestershire was *Tettanbyrig*: Tette was a royal abbess.

The number of women's names indicates that number of personal histories; yet without diaries and letters, we will never know them. Oddly enough, the one place where we do find the words and opinions of early Englishwomen is the dry and dusty field of legal documents. This is because early legal transactions were verbal: folk made statements in front of witnesses. Later, under the influence of Christianity, sworn statements were preserved in writing, with the signatures (or marks, with the names written in by a clerk) of the witnesses. As Englishwomen owned property, they could sell it, exchange it, leave it in their wills; so in their various deeds, testaments and lawsuits they made their claims and wishes known to later generations. For example, when settling her legacies to her four children, the lady Wulfwaru said: "And I grant to my eldest daughter, Gode, the estate at Winford, with produce and people and all profits; and two cups of four pounds and one headband of thirty mancusses of gold and a complete woman's outfit...". This does not tell much about Wulfwaru, except that she had property and a family, but at least she can be heard telling it in her own unadorned English words. The letters of the German mission are distanced by the Latin language and style.

However, there is one report of a legal dispute where personal feeling boils over. This is the only moment in early English records where one can hear a real live Englishwoman – not a poetic heroine – speaking passionately at some length.[47]

One day in the early eleventh century, Edwin son of Enniaunn came to the Hereford shire meeting to lodge a complaint that his widowed mother was keeping wrongful possession of his two estates – Wellington and Cradley – that should have come to him with the rest of his inheritance as eldest son. (Presumably, his mother was claiming that they

---

[47] Edwin's attempt to have the law on his mother (*Anglo-Saxon Charters* No. 78 A. J. Robertson) is No. XII B in *Sweet's Anglo-Saxon Reader* 15th Ed. Revised by Dorothy Whitelock. The passage has notes and a glossary. It has been translated by her in *English Historical Documents Vol. I 500-1042, no. 135.*

There is an extract with translation and comment in *An Invitation to Old English and Anglo-Saxon England* §399 p. 213: Bruce Mitchell, Blackwell 1995; and a comment in *Women in Anglo-Saxon England* ch. 4 Family and Kinship p. 78.

were her personal property and therefore not part of his inheritance.) The shire-reeve nominated three representatives of this assembly, three thanes, to visit the mother and ask her to make good her claim to the disputed lands.

When they told her what they had come for, she was furious with her son: "*and gebealh heo*" literally means "and she swelled with anger"; she bulged! The clerk reporting the hearing described her manner as "very *earlish*" – like an earl. Bruce Mitchell interprets the literal meaning of this magnificent Old English phrase "swiðe eorlice" as angry "in a way fitting for a noble";[48] the emotional equivalent in modern English would be "in a right royal rage".

The clerk started by reporting her statement "– she said that she had no land that in any way belonged to him –". Then he got so carried away by her eloquence that he took it down as it flowed from her lips. Reading it, one can see her as well as hear her, flinging her arm wide in a dramatic gesture:

"Here sits Leofflæd, my kinswoman, and after my death I grant her my land and my gold, my robes and my furnishings and everything I've got!"

Then she said to the thanes (it sounds as if she turned on them!)

"Act like thanes! And repeat exactly what I said, to the moot, in front of all those worthy men, and let them know who I'm leaving my land and all my property, and not a thing to my own son, and ask them to witness this!"

And they did; the record was entered on a blank space at the end of the manuscript of the gospels, which is at Hereford, as witness to an Englishwoman who lived not long before 1066: her wealth, her legal rights – and her determination to use them.

This voice from the past does not sound altogether strange. The Old English words may be unfamiliar. The energetic phrasing, the hypnotic rhythms, the tone of command, the sense that King Alfred is advancing on the Danes at Ethandune – these can all be heard in later English literature. This is the voice of Mrs Quickly having Falstaff arrested for debt; of Mrs Joe Gargery on the rampage; of Mrs Proudie turning the

---

[48] Bruce Mitchell ibid.

Bishop of Barchester into quivering jelly in a couple of sentences. Not shield-maidens but battle-axes.

It is not possible to sum up the subject of women's part in early English society by a resounding final sentence. It could only be a resounding cliché – not only trite but also untrue to those few Englishwomen who have been mentioned here, and the many who have been passed over. There is no conclusion that could be true about them all, from queens to serfs, from virgins to whores. No statement could apply to them all except that they were all Englishwomen.

One Englishwoman managed to act and master nearly every part that was possible for a woman to play in the early Germanic world. In fact, the only thing we are certain she did not do was to lead troops into battle, though she was as intelligent a strategist as Æthelflæd of Mercia, had as cool a head, and certainly needed as much courage and endurance. Her life story can make a place to pause.

In one way her achievement was even greater than Æthelflæd's. King Alfred's daughter would have been a person of some importance even if she had never raised a hand except to beckon a servant to attend her. When first we hear of Balthild,[49] she was not a person at all, legally – because she was a slave, a chattel, a thing. Furthermore, she was a slave in a foreign land, with added handicaps of being an alien: unfamiliar speech and customs, no close bond of sympathy even with her fellow slaves.

[49] Materials for the life of Balthild.

The Merovingian Kingdoms Ian Wood Longman 1994. Balthild's presence needs to be hunted for in the index and the Genealogies (she is on p. 349). The entries are too scattered to make a biography, but they 'place' her in the Merovingian history.
Sainted Women of the Dark Ages ch. 14 *Balthild, Queen of Neustria*. This includes the earliest 'Life' which was written soon after her death. Ed. and trans. Jo Ann McNamara and John E. Halborg, Duke Univ. Press 1992.
Women in Frankish Society: Marriage and the Cloister 500-900 Suzanne Wemple Philadelphia: Univ. of Pennsylvania 1981.
Queens as Jezebels: The Careers of Brunhild and Balthild in Merovingian History: Janet L. Nelson in *Medieval Women* ed. Derek Baker The Ecclesiastical History Society Blackwell 1978.
Life of Wilfrid: Eddius Stephanus Webb and Farmer ch. 6 pp.111-12. The only contemporary English reference to Balthild.
The Franks: Edward James Blackwell 1988 pp.225-26 and Plate 45: the "chemise de Sainte Balthilde".

Balthild had been sold into Neustria, the kingdom of the western Franks. She must have been quality merchandise, as she had been bought for the domestic household of Erchinoald, the mayor of the palace, that is, head of the royal establishment, the chief minister and most powerful man in the kingdom from 640–658.

Now, Balthild's first biographer was a nun at Chelles, the great teaching convent that was the model and inspiration of Hild's Whitby. Hild had planned to join it. Balthild had re-founded it when it was moribund, appointed its brilliant abbess Bertilla, and finally retired to it to end her days in saintliness. So the biographer is understandably discreet about the early stages of Balthild's career. The official, convent-inspired version is that Erchinoald was so struck by her modesty, her care and attention to him, that when his wife died, he wanted to marry her. But Balthild was so otherwordly that she wanted to remain a pure maiden, so she hid herself under a pile of dirty rags and Erchinoald was unable to find her.

This is not a likely story. Would a Frankish war-lord take No from one of his female slaves, and not order the rest of his staff to find and bring her or he would have them flayed alive? And would any intelligent female slave miss the chance to marry the effective head of the government?

The obvious deduction is that, seeing her quality – "outstandingly beautiful and very clever" is a contemporary description of her – Erchinoald decided to groom and train her to catch the king's attention, reasoning that if he controlled the king's mistress he would have a firmer hold on the king. At any rate, she did come to the king's attention and he was so struck by her that he married her, so she moved up socially to being queen-consort of Neustria.

This may sound like a delightful fairytale of a Frankish King Cophetua and the Beggar-maid. History is not so romantic. Merovingian kings had no objection to marrying wives of servile origin. Their own god-born ancestry put them above mere mortals. Also, wives of that class had no powerful, dangerous kin-groups behind them, greedy for power; it was safer to trust them and relax in bed with them. King Clovis II left an unsavoury name in the chronicles. He was in his late teens when he met Balthild; his pastimes are listed as gluttony, drunkenness, fornication and rape. However, these are routine accusations against any medieval king if he went against a chronicler's ecclesiastical policies. If the stories are true, it says a lot for Balthild's charm, as well as her powers of endurance, that Clovis not only married her but stayed married to her. There is no mention of any serious competition from other women.

Whatever his habits, Clovis treated her with great generosity and also showed some thoughtfulness. He chose the saintly Genesius, later archbishop of Lyons as her household chaplain and adviser. Considering the disadvantages of her past and her situation – she had no powerful male kin-group to back her, to threaten trouble if she were discarded or murdered – one might have expected her to react in two ways: to be completely servile to the king, the source of her new-found wealth and status; to pile up so much loot as she could while the good times lasted. She did neither.

Tracing her progress, we can see her building herself an artificial kin-group by establishing a friendly partnership with influential, reforming churchmen, not just in Neustria but in the other Frankish kingdoms of Austrasia and Burgundia. The men chosen as her allies were men of intelligence and education. Some were of genuine holiness: Leodegar (St. Leger), Eligius (St. Eloi) and Audoenus (St. Ouen) as well as St. Genesius.

Balthild used the wealth that was now at her command to found or build up monasteries. It must be remembered that in the seventh century, such establishments were not just islands of peace and comparative security amid the violence, but centres of progressive education and mental liberation for women and men.

They were also a useful counterweight to the urban bishops. The walled Roman towns were local strongpoints in the grip of the local warlord's family; the bishop was usually the brother or other close kinsman of the count, throwing his wealth and authority behind any defiance of the king.

Balthild genuinely cared about education and spiritual discipline, but she also diverted a lot of money and influence to the monastic side of the church. Also, she got her own appointees into the bishoprics. A modern historian says there was "a steely political sense" behind Balthild's gracious unassuming manners. When Erchinoald, with whom she was always on terms of friendly respect, died in 658, Balthild replaced him with Ebroin, who is famous as the most efficient and ruthless political thug in seventh century France. There were some jobs where holiness and scholarship were no use, and mayor of the Palace was one of them.

Clovis died in 657. She had borne him three sons, and now became regent for the eldest, Clothar III, a little boy not yet seven years old.

As regent, she now had political power as well as social status; she used it to tighten up the laws on slave-trading. Clearly, she had never forgotten her early humiliations and was not afraid that others would remember them too. She spent a lot of time, money and thought on redeeming and providing for slaves, especially English slaves.

Therefore it is strange that while French sources, then and now, speak highly of her as a great queen and a good woman – she is Sainte Balthilde in their calendar – the one contemporary English source that mentions her calls her a Jezebel and a murderess. The man who said that was Eddi, known in religion as Stephanus, who wrote Wilfrid's biography. Eddi divided the human race into those who supported Wilfrid and those who gave him trouble. As a young man in 658, Wilfrid had been entertained by the then Bishop of Lyons, Aunemundus. The bishop, together with his brother, Count Dalfinus, the Prefect of Lyons, were accused of treason and summoned to appear in front of the regent and her council. Dalfinus appeared; he was found guilty and executed. The bishop said he was ill and did not come. Balthild sent high-ranking officials (*duces*: dukes) to bring him to the royal court; only if he resisted arrest, they had orders to kill him. The party set out for the court; on the way, the bishop was murdered one night by two armed men. His escort was surprised, shocked and bitterly regretful.

Wilfrid, telling the story years later to Eddi, believed that Balthild had masterminded the execution and the murder. Certainly, she immediately replaced the bishop by one of her own political and religious supporters. This was in the nervous time at the beginning of the boy-king's reign and Balthild's regency. Dalfinus and Aunemundus could well have been planning to make trouble in Burgundy. Balthild, with her own child and kingdom to protect, may well have decided on a pre-emptive strike; if she did not, Ebroin certainly would. However, there is no proof of any of this.

Wilfrid seems to have been caught up in the trouble when the household of Aunemundus was arrested; he told Eddi that his last hour had come. However, the executioners found out in time that he was English. Now there was no way that anyone in England could have known in time that he was in danger, let alone have intervened – one cannot imagine Oswiu launching a naval and military strike from Northumbria to save or avenge him. The only possible English help was the English queen-regent. If the story as Eddi tells it is true – some of his details do not fit – then Wilfrid was not showing a very grateful spirit or leaving a very inspiring memory of Balthild in England.

Certainly, she was no dreamy idealist, living remote from the world of power-politics. She had a good eye for a political chance: in 660, a failed coup in Austrasia removed the male heir, but left his sister as heiress. Balthild moved in at once to make a marriage for her younger son, so bringing Austrasia under her influence. She used her network of church contacts as a true peaceweaver to prevent war between the usually feuding Frankish states. According to the *Liber Historiae Francorum*, she succeeded in establishing "a concord of peace" that was observed among three kingdoms during her regency.

In 665, the regency came to an end, as Clothar was 15, of an age to choose his own advisers. While Balthild was his chief adviser, she would still tell him who to favour, whom to exclude. A group of powerful nobles, led by Ebroin who meant to be the chief adviser himself, organised a coup to get rid of the queen-mother. It was remarkably civilised; the fact that Balthild was not murdered must count as one of her miracles. Just over 50 years earlier, the indomitable old queen-dowager Brunhild came to a ghastly end. Balthild was 'allowed' to retire, as if it had been her own request, to her beloved Chelles, where the abbess was her own nominee.

So began her fourth earthly career as a holy sister. The nun-biographer lays great emphasis on her humility but lets slip that she often gave Abbess Bertilla the benefit of her advice, which was always followed. At Chelles, after her death they kept one of her chemises as a holy relic. It still exists; there is a photograph of it in Edward James's book *The Franks*. It is not sackcloth; it is silk, embroidered in a design to look like Byzantine imperial jewellery.

She took a little god-daughter, Radegund, with her to the convent and cherished her dearly. Perhaps she had always wanted a daughter, to give a better childhood than her own. But when the little girl died at the age of seven, Balthild is said to have remarked that *that was better for the child than being married.*

The good nun who wrote this clearly thought the words proved that Balthild had always been a holy virgin in spirit, even if the facts of her life had been against her. It seems to me that they give a glimpse of what she felt about the sexual humiliations and disgust that had brought her to queenship. Still, a career that began as a foreign slave-girl, then progressed through queen-consort, queen-regent, holy woman to canonised saint, is one that any Englishwoman can be proud of – not a dream, a type or cliché but a complex, intelligent, 'unsinkable' woman.

Bibliography

AERTSEN, HENK & ROLF H. BREMNER, JN: *Companion to Old English Poetry*, VU University Press, Amsterdam 1994.

BACKHOUSE, JANET, D. H. TURNER, LESLIE WEBSTER (ed.): *The Golden Age of Anglo-Saxon Art*, British Museum Publications 1984.

BAKER, DEREK (ed.): *Medieval Women*, Blackwell, Oxford 1978.

BEDE:*Historia Ecclesiastica Gentis Anglorum – H.E.G.A.*: trans. J. E. King; *Bede, Historical Works*, Loeb Classical Library, Heinemann/Harvard U.P.

BRADLEY, S. A. J. (trans. & ed.): *Anglo-Saxon Poetry*, Everyman Classics, Dent 1982.

BRANSTON, BRIAN: *The Lost Gods of England*, Thames & Hudson 1984.

CLEMOES, PETER A. M. (ed.): *The Anglo-Saxons: Studies in Some Aspects of Their History and Culture Presented to Bruce Dickins*, Bowes & Bowes 1959.

CROSSLEY-HOLLAND, KEVIN (trans. & ed.): *The Exeter Riddle Book*, The Folio Society 1978.

DIO, CASSIUS (usually termed 'Dio Cassius' or 'Dio') trans. E Carey: *Dio's Roman History*, Loeb Classical Library, Heinemann/Harvard U.P. 1984.

DRONKE, PETER: *Women Writers of the Middle Ages*, Cambridge U.P. 1984.

EKWALL, E.: *Concise Oxford Dictionary of English Place-Names*, Oxford U.P. 1936; 4th ed. 1960.

EMERTON, E.: *The Letters of St. Boniface*, Columbia U.P. 1940; rep. 1973.

FELL, CHRISTINE: *Women in Anglo-Saxon England*, Colonnade Books, British Museum Publications 1984.

FLORENCE OF WORCESTER: *Chronicon ex Chronicis* (see STEVENSON, JOSEPH).

FORESTER, THOMAS (trans. & ed.): *The Chronicle of Henry of Huntingdon*, 1853; facsimile reprint Llanerch press 1991.

FOULKE, WILLIAM DUDLEY (trans. & ed.): *History of the Lombards: Paul the Deacon*, 1907; reprint Univ. of Pennsylvania Press 1974.

GARMONSWAY, G. N. (trans. & ed.): *The Anglo-Saxon Chronicle*, Everyman's University Library, Dent 1972.

HAMER, RICHARD (trans. With parallel O.E. text & ed.): *A Choice of Anglo-Saxon Verse*, Faber & Faber 1970.

HENRY OF HUNTINGDON: *Historia Anglorum* (see FORRESTER, THOMAS).

HUMBLE, RICHARD: *The Saxon Kings*, Weidenfeld & Nicolson 1980.

JAMES, EDWARD: *The Franks*, Blackwell 1988.

KEYNES, SIMON & MICHAEL LAPIDGE (trans. & ed.): *Alfred the Great: Asser's Life of King Alfred and other contemporary sources*, Penguin Books 1983.

KLAEBER, F. (ed.): *Beowulf* and *The Fight at Finnsburg*, 1922; 3rd ed. with supplements D. C. Heath, Lexington Mass. 1950.

KRAPP, GEORGE PHILIP & ELLIOTT VAN KIRK DOBBIE: *The Exeter Book: The Anglo-Saxon Poetic Records III* (A.S.P.R.), Columbia U.P./Routledge & Kegan Paul 1936.

LESLIE, R. F. (ed.): *Three Old English Elegies*, University of Exeter 1988.

LEVISON, W.: *England and the Continent in the Eighth Century*, Oxford 1946.

MCNAMARA, JO ANN, JOHN E. HALBORG, E. GORDON WHATLEY (trans. & ed.): *Sainted Women of the Dark Ages*, Duke U.P. Durham NC 1992.

MACRAE-GIBSON, O. D. (ed.): *The Old English Riming Poem*, D. S. Brewer 1983.

MAYR-HARTING, HENRY: *The Coming of Christianity to Anglo-Saxon England*, Batsford 1971; 3rd ed. 1991.

MITCHELL, BRUCE: *An Invitation to Old English and Anglo-Saxon England*, Blackwell, Oxford 1995.

NEWARK, TIM: *Women Warlords*, Blandford 1989.

NEWTON, SAM: *The Origins of 'Beowulf' and the Pre-Viking Kingdom of East Anglia*, D. S. Brewer 1993.

NORMAN, F. (ed.): *Waldere*, Methuen 1933.

PAULUS DIACONUS: *Historia Langobardorum* (see FOULKE, WILLIAM DUDLEY).

POLLINGTON, STEPHEN: *The Warrior's Way: England in the Viking Age*, Blandford 1989.

PROCOPIUS trans. H. B. Dewing: *History of the Wars: The Gothic War*, Loeb Classical Library, Harvard/Heinemann 1978.

ROBERTSON, A. J.: *Anglo-Saxon Charters*, Cambridge 1939; reprint 1956.

SHIPPEY, T. A.: *Poems of Wisdom and Learning in Old English*, D. S. Brewer/Rowman & Littlefield 1976.

SIMEK, RUDOLF (trans. Angela Hall): *Dictionary of Northern Mythology* 1984; English translation D. S. Brewer 1993.

STATIUS, PAPINIUS (trans. J. H. Mozley): *Silvae*, Loeb Classical Library 1928.

STENTON, F. M.: *Anglo-Saxon England*, Oxford 1943; 3rd ed. 1971;

— *The Historical Bearing of Place-Name Studies: The Place of Women in Anglo-Saxon Society*, Transactions of the Royal Historical Society 4th series 25 1943; reprinted in *Collected Papers* 1969.

STEVENSON, JOSEPH (trans. & ed.): *Florence of Worcester: A History of the Kings of England*, Seeley 1853; facsimile reprint Llanerch 1989.

— *William of Malmesbury: the Kings before the Norman Conquest*, Seeley 1854; facsimile reprint Llanerch 1991.

STONE, ALBY: *Wyrd: Fate and Destiny in North European Paganism*, Newark 1989; reprinted 1991.

SWANTON, MICHAEL (trans. & ed.): *The Anglo-Saxon Chronicle*, Dent 1996.

TACITUS, CORNELIUS (trans. M. Hutton; rev. E. H. Warmington) *Germania*, Loeb Classical Library 1970.

— (trans. C. E. Moore) *The Histories*, Loeb Classical Library 1931.

TALBOT, C. H.: *The Anglo-Saxon Missionaries on the Continent*, Sheed & Ward 1954.

TIMMER, B. J. (ed.): *Judith*, University of Exeter 1978.

WAINWRIGHT, F. T.: *Æthelflæd, Lady of the Mercians* (see CLEMOES, P)

WEBB, J. F. & D. F. FARMER (trans. & ed.) : *The Age of Bede*, Penguin Books 1988.

WEMPLE, SUZANNE: *Women in Frankish Society: Marriage and the Cloister 500–900*, Univ. of Pennsylvania Press 1981.

WHITLOCK, DOROTHY (trans. & ed.): *Anglo-Saxon Wills*, Cambridge 1930.

— (ed. & rev.): *Sweet's Anglo-Saxon Reader*, Oxford U.P. 1975.

— (trans. & ed.): *English Historical Documents Vol. 1, c.500–1042*, 2nd ed. London 1979.

WHITTOCK, MARTIN J.: *The Origins of England 410–600*, Croom Helm 1986.

WILLIAM OF MALMESBURY: *Gesta Regum Anglorum* (see STEVENSON, JOSEPH).

WILLIAMS, ANN, WILFRID P. SMYTH & D. P. KIRBY: *A biographical Dictionary of Dark Age Britain*, B. A. Seaby 1991.

WOOD, IAN: *The Merovingian Kingdoms 450–751*, Longman 1994.

Some of our other titles

An Introduction to the Old English Language and its Literature
Stephen Pollington

The purpose of this general introduction to Old English is not to deal with the teaching of Old English but to dispel some misconceptions about the language and to give an outline of its structure and its literature. Some basic knowledge about the origins of the English language and its early literature is essential to an understanding of the early period of English history and the present form of the language. This revised and expanded edition provides a useful guide for those contemplating embarking on a linguistic journey.

£4·95   A5   ISBN 1–898281–06–8   64 pages

First Steps in Old English: An easy to follow language course for the beginner
Stephen Pollington

A complete, well presented and easy to use Old English language course that contains all the exercises and texts needed to learn Old English. This course has been designed to be of help to a wide range of students, from those who are teaching themselves at home, to undergraduates who are learning Old English as part of their English degree course. The author is aware that some individuals have little aptitude for learning languages and that many have difficulty with grammar. To help overcome these problems he has adopted a step by step approach that enables students of differing abilities to advance at their own pace. The course includes many exercises designed to aid the learning process. A correspondence course is also available.

£19   ISBN 1-898281-19-X   9½" x 6¾"/245 x 170mm   224 pages

Ærgeweorc: Old English Verse and Prose read by Stephen Pollington

This audiotape cassette can be used in conjunction with *First Steps in Old English* or just listened to for the sheer pleasure of hearing Old English spoken well.

Tracks: 1. Deor. 2. Beowulf – The Funeral of Scyld Scefing. 3. Engla Tocyme (The Arrival of the English). 4. Ines Domas. Two Extracts from the Laws of King Ine. 5. Deniga Hergung (The Danes' Harrying) Anglo-Saxon Chronicle Entry AD997. 6. Durham 7. The Ordeal (Be ðon ðe ordales weddigaþ) 8. Wið Dweorh (Against a Dwarf) 9. Wið Wennum (Against Wens) 10. Wið Wæterælfadle (Against Waterelf Sickness) 11. The Nine Herbs Charm 12. Læcedomas (Leechdoms) 13. Beowulf's Greeting 14. The Battle of Brunanburh 15. Blacmon – by Adrian Pilgrim.

£7·50   ISBN 1–898281–20–3   C40 audiotape   Old English transcript supplied with tape.

Wordcraft: Concise English/Old English Dictionary and Thesaurus
Stephen Pollington

Wordcraft provides Old English equivalents to the commoner modern words in both dictionary and thesaurus formats. Previously the lack of an accessible guide to vocabulary deterred many would-be students of Old English. *Wordcraft* combines the core of indispensable words relating to everyday life with a selection of terms connected with society, culture, technology, religion, perception, emotion and expression to encompass all aspects of Anglo-Saxon experience. The Thesaurus presents vocabulary relevant to a wide range of individual topics in alphabetical lists, thus making it easily accessible to those with specific areas of interest. Each thematic listing is encoded for cross-reference from the Dictionary. The two sections will be of invaluable assistance to students of the language, as well as those with either a general or a specific interest in the Anglo-Saxon period.

£11·95   ISBN 1–898281–02–5   A5   256 pages

Leechcraft: Early English Charms, Plantlore and Healing
Stephen Pollington

An unequalled examination of every aspect of early English healing, including the use of plants, amulets, charms, and prayer. Other topics covered include Anglo-Saxon witchcraft; tree-lore; gods, elves and dwarves.

The author has brought together a wide range of evidence for the English healing tradition, and presented it in a clear and readable manner. The extensive 2,000-entry index makes it possible for the reader to quickly find specific information.

The three key Old English texts are reproduced in full, accompanied by new translations. *Bald's Third Leechbook*; *Lacnunga*; *Old English Herbarium*.

£35 ISBN 1–898281–23–8 10" x 6¾" (254 x 170mm) hardcover 28 illustrations 544 pages

A Guide to Late Anglo-Saxon England: From Alfred to Eadgar II 871–1074
Donald Henson

This guide has been prepared with the aim of providing the general readers with both an overview of the period and a wealth of background information. Facts and figures are presented in a way that makes this a useful reference handbook.

Contents include: The Origins of England; Physical Geography; Human Geography; English Society; Government and Politics; The Church; Language and Literature; Personal Names; Effects of the Norman Conquest. All of the kings from Alfred to Eadgar II are dealt with separately and there is a chronicle of events for each of their reigns. There are also maps, family trees and extensive appendices.

£12·95 ISBN 1–898281–21–1 9½" x 6¾"/245 x 170mm, 6 maps & 3 family trees 208 pages

The English Elite in 1066 - Gone but not forgotten
Donald Henson

The people listed in this book formed the topmost section of the ruling elite in 1066. It includes all those who held office between the death of Eadward III (January 1066) and the abdication of Eadgar II (December 1066). There are 455 individuals in the main entries and these have been divided according to their office or position.

The following information is listed where available:
- What is known of their life;
- Their landed wealth;
- The early sources in which information about the individual can be found
- Modern references that give details about his or her life.

In addition to the biographical details, there is a wealth of background information about English society and government. A series of appendices provide detailed information about particular topics or groups of people.

£16·95 ISBN 1–898281–26–2 250 x 175mm / 10 x 7 inches paperback 272 pages

Looking for the Lost Gods of England
Kathleen Herbert

Kathleen Herbert sifts through the royal genealogies, charms, verse and other sources to find clues to the names and attributes of the Gods and Goddesses of the early English. The earliest account of English heathen practices reveals that they worshipped the Earth Mother and called her Nerthus. The tales, beliefs and traditions of that time are still with us and able to stir our minds and imaginations.

£4·95   ISBN 1–898281–04–1   A5   64 pages

A Handbook of Anglo-Saxon Food: Processing and Consumption
Ann Hagen

For the first time information from various sources has been brought together in order to build up a picture of how food was grown, conserved, prepared and eaten during the period from the beginning of the 5th century to the 11th century. No specialist knowledge of the Anglo-Saxon period or language is needed, and many people will find it fascinating for the views it gives of an important aspect of Anglo-Saxon life and culture. In addition to Anglo-Saxon England the Celtic west of Britain is also covered. Subject headings include: drying, milling and bread making; dairying; butchery; preservation and storage; methods of cooking; meals and mealtimes; fasting; feasting; food shortages and deficiency diseases.

£9·95   ISBN 0–9516209–8–3   A5   192 pages

A Second Handbook of Anglo-Saxon Food & Drink
Production & Distribution
Ann Hagen

This second handbook complements the first and brings together a vast amount of information. Subject headings include: cereal crops; vegetables, herbs and fungi; fruit and nuts; cattle; sheep; goats; pigs; poultry and eggs; wild animals and birds; honey; fish and molluscs; imported food; tabooed food; provision of a water supply; fermented drinks; hospitality and charity. 27-page index.

Food production for home consumption was the basis of economic activity throughout the Anglo-Saxon period and ensuring access to an adequate food supply was a constant preoccupation. Used as payment and a medium of trade, food was the basis of the Anglo-Saxons' system of finance and administration.

£14·95   ISBN 1–898281–12–2   A5   432 pages

Anglo-Saxon Riddles
Translated by John Porter

This is a book full of ingenious characters who speak their names in riddles. Here you will meet a one-eyed garlic seller, a bookworm, an iceberg, an oyster, the sun and moon and a host of others from the everyday life and imagination of the Anglo-Saxons.

John Porter's sparkling translations retain all the vigour and subtly of the original Old English poems, transporting us back over a thousand years to the roots of our language and literature.

This edition contains all 95 riddles of the Exeter Book.

£4·95   ISBN 1–898281–13–0   A5   112 pages

Ordering

Payment may be made by Visa, or Mastercard. Telephone orders accepted.
Payment may also be made by a cheque drawn on a UK bank in sterling.
If you are paying by cheque please make it payable to Anglo-Saxon Books and enclose it with your order. When ordering by post please write clearly.
UK deliveries add 10% up to a maximum of £2·50
Europe – including **Republic of Ireland** - add 10% plus £1 – all orders sent airmail
North America add 10% surface delivery, 30% airmail
Elsewhere add 10% surface delivery, 40% airmail
Overseas surface delivery 6–8 weeks; airmail 5–10 days
For details of other titles and our North American distributor see our website or send a s.a.e. to:

Anglo-Saxon Books

Frithgarth, Thetford Forest Park, Hockwold-cum-Wilton, Norfolk IP26 4NQ England
Tel: +44 (0)1842 828430 Fax: +44 (0)1842 828332
web site www.asbooks.co.uk   e-mail: sales@asbooks.co.uk

Þa Engliscan Gesiðas

Þa Engliscan Gesiðas (The English Companions) is a historical and cultural society exclusively devoted to Anglo-Saxon history. Its aims are to bridge the gap between scholars and non-experts, and to bring together all those with an interest in the Anglo-Saxon period, its language, culture and traditions, so as to promote a wider interest in, and knowledge of all things Anglo-Saxon. The Fellowship publishes a journal, *Wiðowinde,* which helps members to keep in touch with current thinking on topics from art and archaeology to heathenism and Early English Christianity. The Fellowship enables like-minded people to keep in contact by publicising conferences, courses and meetings that might be of interest to its members.

For further details see www.kami.demon.co.uk/gesithas/ or write to: The Membership Secretary, Þa Engliscan Gesiðas, BM Box 4336, London, WC1N 3XX England.

Regia Anglorum

Regia Anglorum is a society that was founded to accurately re-create the life of the British people as it was around the time of the Norman Conquest. Our work has a strong educational slant and we consider authenticity to be of prime importance. We prefer, where possible, to work from archaeological materials and are extremely cautious regarding such things as the interpretation of styles depicted in manuscripts. Approximately twenty-five per cent of our membership, of over 500 people, are archaeologists or historians.

The Society has a large working Living History Exhibit, teaching and exhibiting more than twenty crafts in an authentic environment. We own a forty-foot wooden ship replica of a type that would have been a common sight in Northern European waters around the turn of the first millennium AD. Battle re-enactment is another aspect of our activities, often involving 200 or more warriors.

For further information see www.regia.org or contact: K. J. Siddorn, 9 Durleigh Close, Headley Park, Bristol BS13 7NQ, England, e-mail: kim_siddorn@compuserve.com

Bede's World at Jarrow

Bede's world tells the remarkable story of the life and times of the Venerable Bede, 673–735 AD. Visitors can explore the origins of early medieval Northumbria and Bede's life and achievements through his own writings and the excavations of the monasteries at Jarrow and other sites.

Location – 10 miles from Newcastle upon Tyne, off the A19 near the southern entrance to the River Tyne tunnel. Bus services 526 & 527

Bede's World, Church Bank, Jarrow, Tyne and Wear, NE32 3DY
Tel: 0191 489 2106; Fax: 0191 428 2361; website: www.bedesworld.co.uk

Sutton Hoo near Woodbridge, Suffolk

Sutton Hoo is a group of low burial mounds overlooking the River Deben in south-east Suffolk. Excavations in 1939 brought to light the richest burial ever discovered in Britain – an Anglo-Saxon ship containing a magnificent treasure which has become one of the principal attractions of the British Museum. The mound from which the treasure was dug is thought to be the grave of Rædwald, an early English king who died in 624/5 AD.

This National Trust site has an excellent visitor centre, which includes a reconstruction of the burial chamber and its grave goods. Some of the original artefacts are often on display.

The Sutton Hoo Society

Our aims and objectives focus on promoting research and education relating to the Anglo Saxon Royal cemetery at Sutton Hoo, Suffolk in the UK. The Society publishes a newsletter SAXON twice a year, which keeps members up to date with society activities, carries resumes of lectures and visits, and reports progress on research and publication associated with the site. If you would like to join the Society please write to:

Membership Secretary, Sutton Hoo Society,
258 The Pastures, High Wycombe, Buckinghamshire HP13 5RS England
website: www.suttonhoo.org

West Stow Anglo-Saxon Village

An early Anglo-Saxon Settlement reconstructed on the site where it was excavated consisting of timber and thatch hall, houses and workshop. Open all year 10am–4.15pm (except Yule). Special provision for school parties. A teachers' resource pack is available. Costumed events are held at weekends, especially Easter Sunday and August Bank Holiday Monday. Craft courses are organised.

For further details see www.stedmunds.co.uk/west_stow.html or contact:
The Visitor Centre, West Stow Country Park, Icklingham Road, West Stow,
Bury St Edmunds, Suffolk IP28 6HG Tel: 01284 728718